MW00789639

Sweet and Simple Sewing

Quilts and Sewing Projects to Give—or Keep

JESSI JUNG, CARRIE JUNG, AND LAUREN JUNG

Martingale®
Create with Confidence

Dedication

To our amazing family and friends, with a special thanks to our significant others, Chip, Jon, and Atul. We're grateful for your constant love and support, as well as your reassurance that we can, in fact, meet all of our deadlines. And to our Westie, Rudy, who reminded us of the importance of long walks and a quick game of fetch every now and then.

- - - -- - -- -

Sweet and Simple Sewing:
Quilts and Sewing Projects to Give—or Keep
© 2014 by Jessi Jung, Carrie Jung, and Lauren Jung

Martingale®
19021 120th Ave. NE, Ste. 102
Bothell, WA 98011-9511 USA
ShopMartingale.com

No part of this product may be reproduced in any form, unless otherwise stated, in which case reproduction is limited to the use of the purchaser. The written instructions, photographs, designs, projects, and patterns are intended for the personal, noncommercial use of the retail purchaser and are under federal copyright laws; they are not to be reproduced by any electronic, mechanical, or other means, including informational storage or retrieval systems, for commercial use. Permission is granted to photocopy patterns for the personal use of the retail purchaser. Attention teachers: Martingale encourages you to use this book for teaching, subject to the restrictions stated above.

The information in this book is presented in good faith, but no warranty is given nor results guaranteed. Since Martingale has no control over choice of materials or procedures, the company assumes no responsibility for the use of this information.

Printed in China
19 18 17 16 15 14   8 7 6 5 4 3 2 1

Library of Congress Cataloging-in-Publication Data is available upon request.

ISBN: 978-1-60468-359-2

Mission Statement

Dedicated to providing quality products and service to inspire creativity.

Credits

PRESIDENT AND CEO: Tom Wierzbicki
EDITOR IN CHIEF: Mary V. Green
DESIGN DIRECTOR: Paula Schlosser
MANAGING EDITOR: Karen Costello Soltys
ACQUISITIONS EDITOR: Karen M. Burns
TECHNICAL EDITOR: Nancy Mahoney
COPY EDITOR: Melissa Bryan
PRODUCTION MANAGER: Regina Girard
COVER AND INTERIOR DESIGNER: Adrienne Smitke
PHOTOGRAPHER: Brent Kane
ILLUSTRATOR: Christine Erikson

Contents

4 Saving the World, One Project at a Time . . .

5 Tools of the Trade

7 Quiltmaking Basics

The Projects

13 Easy Appliqué Pot Holder

17 Luggage Tag

19 Gypsy Moth Quilt

25 Pleats-A-Plenty Clutch

31 Hand-Bound Journal

37 Big Bang Quilt

43 Pencil Box Quilt

49 Curling Iron Cozy

53 Fly-Away Canvases: Andy Warhol–Style

57 He Loves Me Daisy Quilt

63 Makeup Bag

67 Celebrations Quilt

75 Berry Pillow and Pincushion

80 About the Authors

Saving the World, One Project at a Time . . .

Well, maybe the projects in this book won't solve all of today's big problems, but we *do* believe that art and beauty go a long way toward making the world a better place.

Creating beautiful items through sewing and quilting is an art form and your fabric is your paint. With so many designs and styles to choose from, the project possibilities are truly endless. As fabric designers, the desire to experiment with fabric is in our blood, and we'll find any excuse to try out a new sewing project. Sometimes our experiments are successful . . . and sometimes they're not. But for this book, *Sweet and Simple Sewing,* we've included some of our favorite successes, along with a few words of wisdom we've learned along the way.

As you make your way through *Sweet and Simple Sewing,* you'll find a variety of quilting projects—both pieced and appliquéd—to cozy up to, along with instructions for many useful home-decor items, personal accessories, and even a hand-bound journal.

We also hope to show you that you don't need to be a master quilter or sewist to create some great things. You'll find projects here to suit all skill levels, but the truth is, most anyone can complete them all. If you like a project, but feel your skill may not be up to snuff yet, I say try it! Remember, your seam ripper is your friend. Learn to love it.

~ *Carrie*

Tools of the Trade

My quilting studio is relatively new. I love it. I live in it. Sometimes I even sleep in it! But it wasn't always a quilting studio. It evolved. This generic room served many purposes over the years. When my husband and I moved into our home, it started out as a storage area, kind of like an attic. Later it became a spare bedroom with just the bare essentials for a houseguest.

Then came the kids. So the room transformed to a playroom with toys, games, and play kitchens. But kids grow up. They date and entertain friends, so out with the toys and in with a TV, movies, computers, and comfortable furniture. Then the kids leave home. Enter sewing machine, cutting table, books, and patterns, giving me a much-needed sewing room. And just a few months ago, I remodeled that sewing room into a well-appointed quilting studio. I'll admit I am a bit spoiled by it; but the truth is, you can sew and create just about anywhere—kitchen tables and couches included! Because, really, it's all about having the right tools, and that's what this section is all about.

~ Jessi

My favorite room in the house! ~ Jessi

A QUILTER'S TOOL KIT

Below is a list of the basics that we can't do without.

- Sewing machine
- Sewing-machine needles
- Hand-sewing needles
- Sewing thread
- Quilting thread
- Ironing board
- Iron
- Rotary cutter
- Cutting mat
- Quilter's rulers
- Tape measure
- Scissors
- Paper
- Seam ripper
- Curved safety pins
- Straight pins
- Water-soluble marking pen
- Masking tape for basting
- Compass for drafting curves and circles

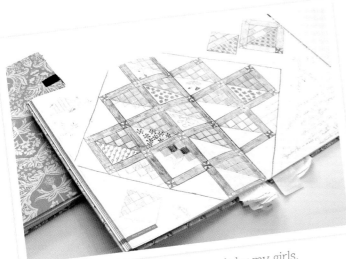

My sketchbook, handmade by my girls, Lauren and Carrie ~ Jessi

ADDITIONAL SUPPLIES WE USE

Here's a list of some not-so-common tools that we also love and use in this book.

Staple gun and staples. These are essential for stapling into wood, as in "Fly-Away Canvases: Andy Warhol–Style" on page 53.

Cording. We use cording for embellishments.

Doll-making needles. These needles are longer and stronger than regular needles, so you can more easily sew through multiple layers when making projects such as pillows and pincushions.

Monofilament, or invisible thread. Use this type of thread when you want your stitches to be virtually unnoticeable.

Fabric-covered button kit. This handy kit allows you to create matching customized buttons for your projects.

Decorative buttons. Specialty buttons offer another way to embellish and personalize your projects.

Methyl cellulose powder. This powder is used in making bookbinding glue and can be hard to find. You may find it at art-supply stores, or it is widely available online.

Book board. Found in most craft stores, this bookbinding basic is a must for making book covers.

Artist's canvas. Canvas stretched on a wooden frame is a great, inexpensive display method for quilt blocks and appliqué patterns—and no batting is required.

Sobo glue. We use this to make bookbinding glue, but this nontoxic adhesive has a variety of other crafty uses as well.

Lint brush. Aside from removing lint from your projects, a lint brush will clean a rotary-cutting mat and pick up all loose bits of thread from seam ripping. We also use it in preparation for quilting to remove dark threads from batting and backing layers that may show through.

Coffee filters. These make great stabilizers because they're inexpensive, readily available, and easy to tear away.

THINGS THAT MAKE LIFE EASIER

And then there are some things we use to make life easier.

Precuts: Using precut fabrics can save you hours of concentration and cutting time.

Ott Lite: A light source that is similar to sunlight, with no glare or heat. Great for nighttime sewing (something we find ourselves doing a lot of).

Design wall: Great for auditioning design choices. While the floor can be an adequate space to try out color combinations and block arrangements, there's something about auditioning your designs on a vertical surface that makes all the difference. You can always buy a design wall, but they are very simple and cheap to make using a large piece of white flannel or a sheet of batting. You can also find instructions online for making a more permanent design wall.

Paper-backed fusible web: Used for fusing an appliqué shape to its foundation. You just trace a shape on the paper side, and cut it out. The webbing adheres to the back of an appliqué piece, and then sticks to the foundation when heated with an iron. It prevents edges from fraying.

Stabilizer: Helps make fabric stronger when sewing, so you can make smooth and even stitches. Stabilizer is pinned underneath an appliqué shape and torn away after the stitching is completed.

Freezer paper: Great for tracing and cutting out designs, it has a waxy side that will stick to fabric when ironed, and it can be removed and reused several times.

Mini ironing board: Save on floor space and are portable. They are perfect for small projects.

Magnetic wand: Perfect for finding and capturing a dropped needle or pin.

Digital camera: Invaluable for everything from auditioning and comparing fabric combinations to sharing new projects. Phone cameras are obviously portable, so wherever you may find inspiration, you can just snap and go.

Quiltmaking Basics

"Measure twice, cut once" may be an old woodworking adage, but frankly, I see it as what baking Christmas cookies taught me about quilting.

~ Jessi

Cutting fabric into precise dimensions of squares, triangles, and other shapes always reminds me of baking. Pattern directions aren't much different from recipes. You press your fabric, similar to rolling out cookie dough, and you arrange templates on cloth much like arranging cookie cutters on the dough. The point is, if you're not exact with your measurements, it will affect the outcome. If you're sloppy with measuring your ingredients, you risk ruining the recipe. So take the time to measure, cut, sew, and press with accuracy. In the end, it will make all the difference between just "good enough" and "well done!"

HALF-SQUARE-TRIANGLE UNITS

Half-square-triangle units consist of two triangles sewn together to make a square. To make a half-square-triangle unit, we find it's easier to begin with two squares, one of each fabric, rather than cutting individual triangles. The basic math for creating these units involves starting with squares that are ⅞" larger than the desired finished size of the half-square-triangle unit. For example, if you need a unit that is 3" finished, you'll start with 3⅞" squares. To play it safe, you can cut your squares 1" larger than the finished size of the half-square-triangle unit, and then trim your unit to the proper size afterward. Just align the seam line on the half-square-triangle unit with the diagonal line on your square ruler, and trim your unit to the correct size.

1. Layer two squares right sides together. Using a pencil, draw a diagonal line across the top square from corner to corner.

2. Sew ¼" from each side of the drawn line. Cut the squares apart on the drawn lines to make two half-square-triangle units. Flip the units open and press the seam allowances in the direction indicated in the project instructions.

MACHINE APPLIQUÉ

We prefer to appliqué and machine quilt using 100% cotton thread or monofilament. Monofilament (also called invisible thread) is made of 100% transparent nylon or polyester, and is available in both clear and smoke hues. Smoke is better for dark fabric colors, and clear is best for light colors. Monofilament is a perfect choice when you want your stitches to be "invisible." We suggest using it on the top of your machine, with regular sewing thread in the bobbin.

Preparation

There are many brands of fusible web on the market. Whichever brand you choose, take time to read the manufacturer's instructions.

In this book, all of the asymmetrical patterns have already been reversed for fusible appliqué. However, if you need to make a reversed image, trace the appliqué pattern onto a piece of paper; then place the paper on a light box or against a bright window, with the traced side toward the light. Trace the shape onto the back of the paper using a black permanent pen.

1. Trace your pattern onto the paper side of the fusible web. Roughly cut out the fusible-web shape, leaving a margin of about ¼" all around the traced line.

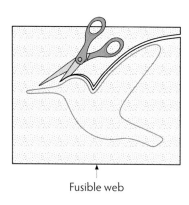

Fusible web

2. Place the fusible-web side of the shape on the wrong side of your fabric. Following the manufacturer's instructions, fuse the shape to the fabric.

3. Cut out the fabric shape on the drawn line and remove the paper backing. Position the appliqué shape, adhesive side down, on the right side of your background fabric and press.

Stitching

Stitching around appliqué shapes will secure the edges. This is usually done with a zigzag, satin, or blanket stitch.

1. Place stabilizer underneath your background fabric before stitching. If you purchase a stabilizer product, be sure to follow the manufacturer's instructions.

2. Change your sewing-machine needle to a size 70/10 or 75/11, since a smaller needle will make a smaller hole in the fabric. Set your machine to the "needle down" position, if possible. Always practice your stitching on a scrap piece of fabric to decide if you like the size of the stitches, and to perfect your technique before appliquéing on your actual project!

3. Stitch around the raw edges of your appliqué. (Don't be afraid to lift your presser foot and pivot regularly when sewing around curved edges.) Start and stop with a backstitch to prevent unraveling. Gently tear away the stabilizer.

BORDERS

Border strips are usually cut across the fabric width from selvage to selvage. If the fabric isn't wide enough to fit the sides of your quilt, you'll need to join strips end to end to achieve the desired length. We piece our borders using a straight-of-grain seam, rather than a diagonal seam, because sewing on the bias may cause excess stretching. All border measurements in this book are already calculated for you, but it's a good idea to measure your quilt top through the center before cutting your strips, just to be sure.

1. Fold the quilt top in half and finger-press to mark the center along both sides. Fold the border strips in half and finger-press to mark the centers.

2. Pin the side borders to the quilt, matching the center marks and ends. Sew the borders in place and press the seam allowances toward the borders.

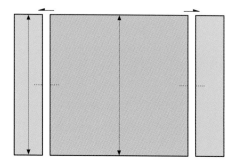

3. Repeat the process for the top and bottom borders.

BACKING

Your backing must be larger than your quilt top. A good rule of thumb is to add 6" to the length and width of your quilt-top measurement. This will give you 3" extra on all four sides. Many times you'll need to piece the backing to make it large enough for your quilt top. We prefer to cut the backing fabric lengthwise, so the seam runs vertically along the length of the quilt. All the backing yardages listed with the projects are sufficient to allow for cutting the fabric lengthwise.

1. Determine how many 42"-wide pieces you'll need across the width for your backing. Then cut each piece to the length of your quilt, plus 6".
2. Trim off the selvages and sew the pieces together using a ½" seam allowance.
3. Press the seam allowances open and cut off any excess backing fabric, making sure to include the extra 6" of length and width.

THE QUILTING PROCESS

A quilt is composed of three layers: the quilt top, batting, and backing. Hand or machine stitches hold the layers together.

The Quilt Sandwich

Before you can start quilting, the quilt top, batting, and backing need to be made into a sandwich and basted together so that the layers don't shift.

1. Lay the backing, wrong side up, on a large, flat surface. Anchor the backing with strips of masking tape around the perimeter, placing them every 5" or so. Pull on the tape to make sure the backing is taut and wrinkle-free. Remove any loose or dark threads with a lint roller to prevent them from showing through the fabric.
2. Lay the batting over the backing, smoothing out any wrinkles.
3. Center the quilt top, right side up, on top of the batting. Smooth out any wrinkles.
4. Use curved safety pins to baste the layers together, working from the center outward.

You can remove the tape strips after pin basting about every 5" on the quilt.

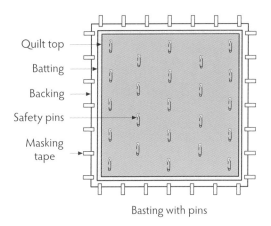

Basting with pins

Simple Machine Quilting

A walking foot is great for quilting in the ditch or quilting simple straight-line patterns because the foot moves up and down, "walking" across the fabric rather than sliding along it. This means your layers of fabric and batting don't bunch up as you quilt. To quilt in the ditch, simply stitch along the seam lines of each quilt block. Begin your quilting in the center of the project and work out toward the edges.

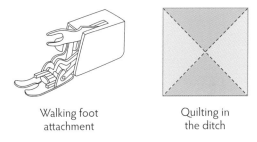

Walking foot attachment

Quilting in the ditch

Free-Motion Quilting

Free-motion quilting allows you to be a little more creative, freeing you from the confines of straight lines and gentle curves. For this type of quilting, you'll need a darning foot and the ability to lower the feed dogs on your machine. Feed dogs are the metal teeth under the presser foot that grip the fabric and move it forward and backward. A darning foot jumps up and down, releasing pressure on the fabric so that you're free to move the quilt layers under the needle.

1. Begin by attaching the darning foot to your machine and lowering the feed dogs.

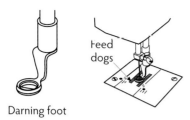

Darning foot

2. Position the quilt under the presser foot. On the first stitch, pull the bobbin thread up to the top surface. Sew two or three stitches in the same place to anchor the thread. Then move the quilt to begin making your pattern. Remember, without the feed dogs, the only way your quilt will move under the needle is if you push it. We recommend practicing on scrap fabric first to get the feel of free-motion machine quilting before stitching your quilt. With practice, you can stitch almost any pattern onto your quilt, from flowers and bees to feathers and leaves.

HANGING SLEEVE

A hanging sleeve is essentially a rod pocket that is attached to the back of a quilt. You can slide a dowel or curtain rod through the sleeve for hanging your quilt on a wall. If you decide to add a hanging sleeve, do so before you attach your binding to the quilt. We like to make the sleeve from the same fabric as our backing, but you can use any leftover fabric that you happen to have.

1. Cut a strip 8" wide by the width of your quilt. Fold the short ends under ½", and then ½" again to make a hem. Stitch in place.

2. Fold the strip in half lengthwise, wrong sides together. Center and baste the raw edges to the top of the quilt back. The top edge of the sleeve will be secured when the binding is sewn to the quilt. The raw edges of the sleeve and quilt will be hidden when you hand sew the binding to the quilt back.

3. Finish the sleeve after the binding has been attached by blindstitching the bottom of

the sleeve to the quilt back. Push the bottom edge of the sleeve up just a bit to provide a little give; this will keep the hanging rod from pulling on the quilt.

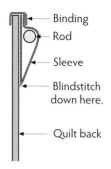

BINDING

Binding consists of strips of fabric that cover the raw edges and encase all three layers of the quilt. We use double-fold straight-grain binding unless the project has curved or zigzagged edges. We cut 2"-wide strips for our binding. If you prefer *bias* binding, simply cut 2"-wide strips on a 45° angle to the selvage instead of across the width of the fabric from selvage to selvage. Otherwise the steps for attaching and finishing the binding are the same.

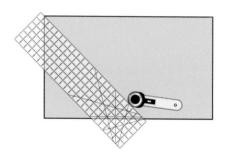

1. Cut the binding strips as instructed for each project. Place the strips right sides together at right angles and draw a 45° line across the top strip as shown. Stitch on the drawn line. Trim the excess fabric, leaving ¼" for seam allowance, and press the seam allowances open.

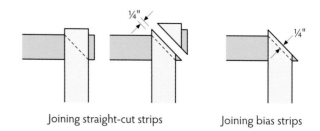

Joining straight-cut strips   Joining bias strips

2. Press the strip in half lengthwise, wrong sides together and raw edges aligned.

3. Trim the batting and backing so the edges are even with the quilt top.

4. Starting in the middle on one side, place an end of the binding strip on the right side of the quilt, aligning the raw edges of the binding strip with the quilt-top edge. Begin stitching about 6" from the start of the binding, using a ¼" seam allowance. Stop sewing ¼" from the first corner and backstitch. Remove the quilt from the machine.

5. Fold the binding straight up so that the fold creates a 45° angle. Bring the binding back down onto itself, even with the raw edge of the quilt top. Beginning at the fold with a backstitch, stitch along the edge of the quilt top, stopping ¼" from the next corner as before.

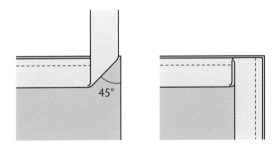

6. Repeat the process on the remaining edges and corners of the quilt.

7. Stop stitching approximately 6" from the starting end of the binding strip. Remove the quilt from the machine. To join the binding ends, place the quilt on a flat surface and overlap the beginning and ending binding tails. Trim the tails so they overlap exactly 2", or the same width as your binding strips. (If your binding strip is 2¼" wide, your overlap would be 2¼".)

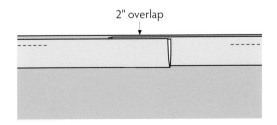

2" overlap

8. Unfold the binding ends and place them right sides together, perpendicular to one another. Pin in place. Draw a diagonal line from corner to corner as shown, and then stitch on the drawn line. Before trimming, make sure the binding is the correct length to fit your quilt and that the seam was sewn in the correct direction! When you're satisfied, trim the excess corner fabric, leaving a ¼" seam allowance. Press the seam allowances open.

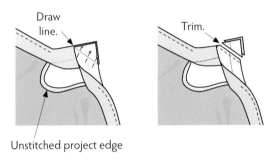

Draw line. Trim.

Unstitched project edge

9. Refold the binding, position it along the quilt, and finish stitching it in place.

10. Fold the binding over the raw edges to the quilt back, with the folded edge covering the row of machine stitching. Hand stitch the binding in place. When you reach a corner, sew just beyond the machine-stitched corner. Fold the next side to form a mitered corner. Tack the miter in place, and continue stitching.

Quilt back

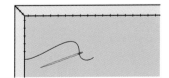

Hand stitch binding to quilt back.

Easy Appliqué Pot Holder

FINISHED SIZE: 8½" x 8½"

Designed and made by Carrie Jung

If you think about it, a pot holder is like a mini-quilt. So if you're new to the quilting and appliqué world, this is a great place to start. You can learn the basics of appliqué, quilting, and binding on a small scale.

MATERIALS

Yardage is based on 42"-wide fabric unless otherwise noted. Yields 1 pot holder.

⅓ yard of fabric A for background, hanging tab, and backing
⅛ yard of fabric B for binding
Assorted scraps, at least 6" x 7", for appliqués
8½" x 8½" square of insulated batting
8" x 8" square of fusible web
8" x 8" square of stabilizer
Matching thread for machine appliqué

CUTTING

From fabric A, cut:
2 squares, 8½" x 8½"
1 strip, 2" x 5"

From fabric B, cut:
1 strip, 2" x 42"

APPLIQUÉING THE POT HOLDER

1. Fold one of the fabric A squares in half vertically and press a light crease along the center fold. Unfold the square and then refold it in half horizontally. Press a light crease to establish centering lines.

If you're in love with your fabric print and can't bear to cover it up with an appliqué shape, then don't! Just skip right to the assembly section of the instructions. Sometimes less is more.

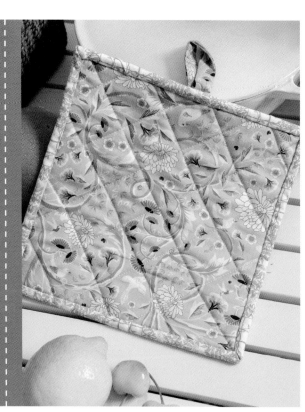

2. Referring to "Machine Appliqué" on page 7, choose from the beehive and flower patterns on page 15 and prepare the shapes for fusible appliqué. Layer the shapes in numerical order onto the background square and fuse in place.

3. Center and pin a piece of stabilizer to the back of the square. Stitch around each shape using a blanket stitch and matching thread. Gently remove the stabilizer.

ASSEMBLING THE POT HOLDER

1. Place the remaining fabric A square wrong side up on a flat surface. Add the insulated batting square, and then place the appliquéd square on top of the batting, right side up. Align the edges and pin the layers together. Quilt as desired.

2. Using a rotary cutter and ruler, trim and square up the edges of the quilted square.

3. To make the tab, press the 2" x 5" strip in half lengthwise, right sides together. Sew along

the long edge, using a ¼" seam allowance. Turn the tab right side out and press.

4. Fold the tab in half, overlapping the ends. On the back of the quilted square, center the tab on the top edge, aligning the raw edges, and baste in place.

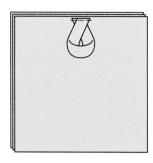

5. Referring to "Binding" on page 10 and using the fabric B 2"-wide strip, make and attach the binding.

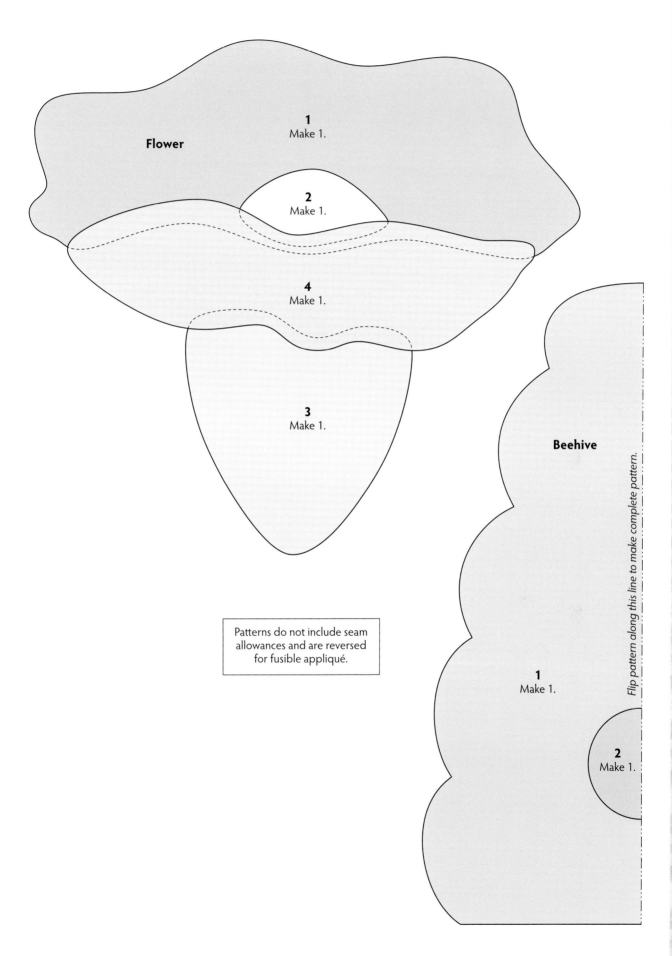

Flower

1
Make 1.

2
Make 1.

4
Make 1.

3
Make 1.

Beehive

1
Make 1.

2
Make 1.

Patterns do not include seam
allowances and are reversed
for fusible appliqué.

Flip pattern along this line to make complete pattern.

LAUREN & JESSI JUNG

Luggage Tag

FINISHED SIZE: 3½" x 3½"

Designed and made by Carrie Jung

We all have baggage. So why not set your suitcase apart from the sea of look-alike luggage? Dazzle all of your fellow passengers and TSA agents with your craftiness.

MATERIALS

Yields 1 luggage tag.

2 squares, 4" x 4", of fabric for tag front and back
4" x 4" square of medium-weight fusible interfacing
4" x 4" square of heavy-duty fusible web
3¼" x 4" rectangle of 20-gauge clear vinyl
⅓ yard of ⅜"-wide ribbon in coordinating color
1 eyelet, ⁵⁄₃₂", and setting tool
Pinking rotary blade

ASSEMBLING THE LUGGAGE TAG

1. Using a dry iron, fuse the square of interfacing to one fabric square, following the manufacturer's instructions. Then fuse the square of fusible web to the remaining fabric square, following the manufacturer's instructions.

2. Remove the paper backing from the fusible web and layer the two prepared squares, *wrong sides together*. Using the wool setting on your iron, fuse the two squares together.

3. Align the long edge of the vinyl rectangle with the bottom of the fused square. Using a ¾"-wide seam allowance, stitch down one side, across the bottom, and up the other side, starting and stopping with a backstitch or two. *Do not* pin the vinyl in place as the pins will leave holes. It's OK if the vinyl shifts a little while stitching; you'll square it up in the next step.

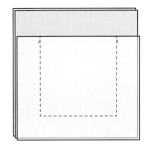

Decorative stitches can add a little something extra to your one-of-a-kind luggage tag. The tags look best made with large prints and calm fabrics.

4. Use the pinking rotary blade to trim ¼" from each side, leaving ½" to ⅝" of fabric extending beyond the seam line on the sides and bottom and ½" of fabric beyond the edge of the vinyl along the top edge.

5. Center the eyelet along the top of the tag ¼" from the top of the vinyl and 1¾" in from the side edge. Follow the manufacturer's instructions to affix the eyelet to the tag.

6. Write your identifying information on a piece of paper and insert it into the tag. Cut a 10" length of ribbon and string it through the eyelet and then through the handle of your favorite piece of luggage. Knot the ends together to secure.

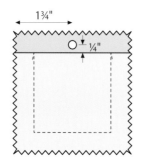

Gypsy Moth Quilt

FINISHED QUILT SIZE: 54½" x 54½"
FINISHED BLOCK SIZE: 9" x 9"

Designed and made by Jessi Jung;
quilted by Judy Howard

Moths sometimes get a bad rap. Yes, they occasionally wreak havoc on your clothing, but if you look beyond that, you'll find that some of them are actually quite beautiful. So here's our nod to the butterfly's less-flashy sister.

MATERIALS

Yardage is based on 42"-wide fabric unless otherwise noted.

1 Layer Cake *OR* 42 squares, 10" x 10", of assorted prints for moth wing appliqués
2⅔ yards of white solid for block backgrounds and first, third, and fifth borders
½ yard of tan check for moth body appliqués
¼ yard of yellow print for second border
¼ yard of blue print for fourth border
½ yard of red print for binding
4 yards of fabric for backing
61" x 61" piece of batting
5 yards of 16"-wide fusible web
4¾ yards of 20"-wide stabilizer
Blue thread for appliqué

CUTTING

From the *lengthwise grain* of the white solid, cut:
2 strips, 1" x 36½"
2 strips, 1" x 37½"
2 strips, 1½" x 39½"
2 strips, 1½" x 41½"
4 strips, 6½" x 42½"

From the remaining white solid, cut:
4 strips, 9½" x 42"; cut into 16 squares, 9½" x 9½"
4 squares, 6½" x 6½"

From the yellow print, cut:
2 strips, 1½" x 37½"
2 strips, 1½" x 39½"

From the blue print, cut:
5 strips, 1" x 42"

From the red print, cut:
6 strips, 2" x 42"

From the stabilizer, cut:
4 strips, 6½" x 42½"
16 squares, 9½" x 9½"
4 squares, 6½" x 6½"

MAKING THE BLOCKS

1. Referring to "Machine Appliqué" on page 7 and using the pattern on page 23, prepare 56 moth wings and 56 moth bodies for fusible appliqué. Fuse moth wings onto the wrong side of each print 10" square. (You'll need to fuse two moth wings on 14 of the squares, so position those fusible-web shapes in opposite corners of the square.) Fuse the moth bodies onto the wrong side of the tan check. Cut out the appliqué shapes directly on the traced lines.

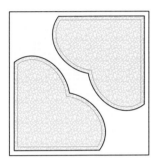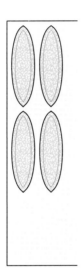

2. Using moth wings from two different prints, position the wings in opposite corners of a white 9½" square, placing them ½" from the raw edges of the square as shown. Place a body in the center of each wing. Fuse the shapes in place. Repeat to make a total of 16 blocks. Set aside the remaining appliqué shapes for the outer border.

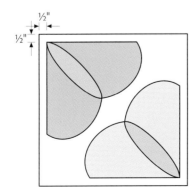

Make 16.

Removing the Paper

After fusing, you can remove stubborn paper backing from your fusible web by stretching or crumbling the piece slightly. The fabric will stretch and the paper will start to tear or pop off.

3. Center and pin a 9½" square of stabilizer to the back of each white square. Stitch around each shape using a blanket stitch and blue thread. Gently remove the stabilizer.

APPLIQUÉING THE BORDER

1. Fold each white 6½"-wide strip in half and lightly press to establish centering creases. Measure 7" from the center crease and press a second fold line. Then measure 7" from the second fold line and press a third fold line. Repeat the process on the other half of the strip. You should have five fold lines, 7" apart.

Center

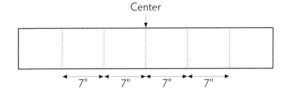

2. Fuse five moth appliqués onto each white strip, centering the pieces on the folded lines as shown. Set aside the four remaining moth appliqués; they will be fused to the border corners after the quilt top is assembled.

3. Center and pin a strip of stabilizer to the back of each white strip. Stitch around each shape using a blanket stitch and blue thread. Gently remove the stabilizer.

ASSEMBLING THE QUILT TOP

1. Arrange the blocks in four rows of four blocks each as shown in the quilt assembly diagram at right. Sew the blocks together into rows. Press the seam allowances in opposite directions from row to row. Sew the rows together and press the seam allowances in one direction.

2. Sew white 1" x 36½" strips to opposite sides of the quilt top. Press the seam allowances toward the strips. Sew white 1" x 37½" strips to the top and bottom. Press the seam allowances toward the strips.

3. Sew yellow 1½" x 37½" strips to opposite sides of the quilt top. Sew yellow 1½" x 39½" strips to the top and bottom. Press all seam allowances toward the yellow strips.

4. Sew white 1½" x 39½" strips to opposite sides of the quilt top. Sew white 1½" x 41½" strips to the top and bottom of the quilt. Press all seam allowances toward the white strips.

5. Join the blue 1"-wide strips end to end. From the pieced strip, cut two 41½"-long strips and sew them to opposite sides of the quilt top. From the remaining pieced strip, cut two 42½"-long strips and sew them to the top and bottom. Press all seam allowances toward the blue strips.

6. Sew appliquéd border strips to opposite sides of the quilt top, making sure the center moth

is facing toward the quilt. Press the seam allowances toward the white strips.

7. Sew a white 6½" square to each end of the two remaining appliquéd border strips. Press the seam allowances toward the strips. Sew the borders to the top and bottom of the quilt top and press.

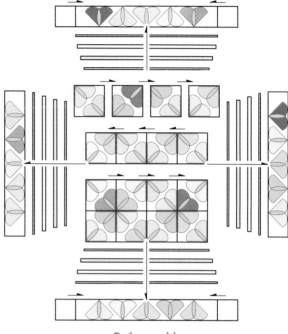

Quilt assembly

8. Refer to the photo above left for placement guidance. On each corner of the outer border, fuse a moth shape 1½" in from both edges of the quilt, making sure the moth is facing away from the quilt center. Center and pin a 6½" square of stabilizer to the back of each appliqué and stitch around the shapes, in the same manner as before. Gently remove the stabilizer.

FINISHING

Refer to the sections "Backing" through "Binding" on pages 9–11 for help with the following finishing techniques as needed.

1. Cut and piece the backing fabric, and then layer the quilt top with batting and backing. Baste the layers together.

2. Quilt as desired.

3. Using the red 2"-wide strips, make and attach the binding.

Moth wing
Make 56 from
assorted prints.

Patterns do not include
seam allowances.

Moth body
Make 56 from
tan check.

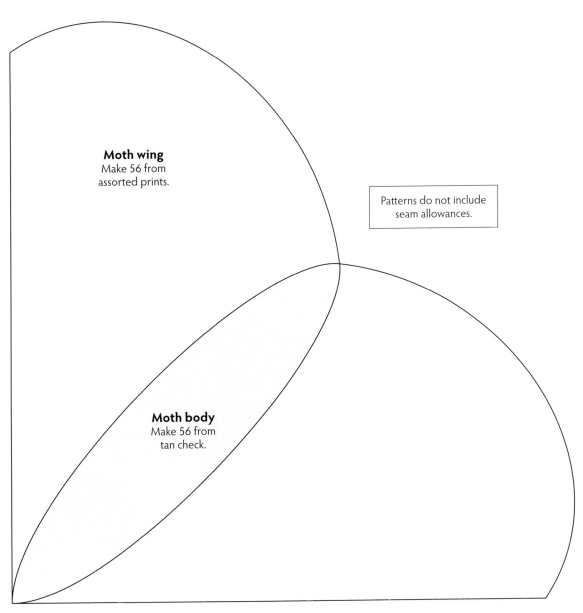

Pleats-A-Plenty Clutch

FINISHED SIZE: 9" x 7½"

Designed and made by Carrie Jung

Don't let the pleats in this project scare you away. Once you get the hang of them, they're a cinch to make, plus they have a way of transforming your favorite fabric into something completely new and quirky.

MATERIALS

Yardage is based on 42"-wide fabric unless otherwise noted.

1⅛ yards of blue print for clutch body
¼ yard of multicolored floral for lining
¼ yard of orange print for top band, interior pocket, and zipper tabs
⅛ yard of teal print for flower embellishment
¾ yard of 22"-wide medium-weight fusible interfacing
9"-long zipper
Fabric-marking pen
Compass for drawing circles

CUTTING

From the blue print, cut:
3 strips, 12" x 42"; cut *1 of the strips* into 2 strips, 12" x 21"

From the multicolored floral, cut:
2 rectangles, 6¾" x 10"
2 rectangles, 2¾" x 10"

From the orange print, cut:
2 rectangles, 2¾" x 10"
2 rectangles, 1½" x 2"
1 rectangle, 4" x 4½"

From the interfacing, cut:
4 rectangles, 6¾" x 10"
4 rectangles, 2¾" x 10"
1 rectangle, 2" x 4½"

MAKING THE CLUTCH BODY

1. With right sides together, join a blue 12" x 42" strip and a blue 12" x 21" strip end to end to make a strip approximately 62" long. Press the seam allowances open. Repeat to make a second pieced strip.

2. Place one pieced strip on your ironing board, right side up. Use a fabric marking pen to draw a vertical line 1" in from the left end of the strip.

Mark line 1" from end.

3. Fold the strip along the line, wrong sides together, placing the folded edge about ⅜" from the left end of the strip to make a pleat. Press the pleat.

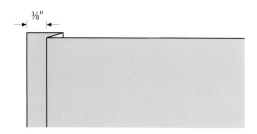

4. With wrong sides together, fold about 1" of fabric and place the fold to the left to form a second pleat. The folded edge should be about ⅛" from the first pleat. Press.

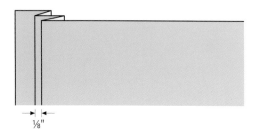

5. Continue pleating in the same way, alternating the width of the pleats as shown, until the pleated strip is about 12" to 13" long. When you reach the seam, adjust the fold so that the seam is underneath a pleat, making sure to keep a uniform amount of space between the pleats.

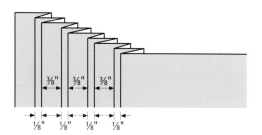

6. Place the pleated strip *wrong* side up on your ironing board, with the pleats positioned vertically. Make sure the pleated lines are straight. Center a 6¾" x 10" rectangle of interfacing on top of the pleated strip. Follow the manufacturer's instructions to fuse the interfacing to the strip. Carefully machine baste around the edges of the interfacing using a ¼" seam allowance. Trim the edges of the pleated strip even with the interfacing. The piece should measure 6¾" x 10".

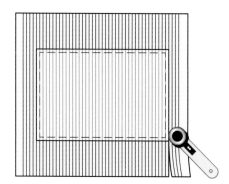

7. Flip the piece over and use a fabric marking pen to draw a horizontal line 2¼" from the top edge. Draw a second horizontal line 2¼" from the bottom edge. Topstitch along the lines. When topstitching, always feed the pleated piece through the machine with the folds facing toward you so that they don't catch on the presser foot.

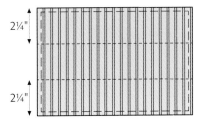

8. Repeat steps 2–7 to make a second pleated piece.

9. Follow the manufacturer's instructions to fuse a 2¾" x 10" rectangle of interfacing to the wrong side of each orange 2¾" x 10" rectangle. Pin an orange rectangle to the top of one pleated piece, right sides together and raw edges aligned as shown. Using a ½" seam allowance, sew the pieces together, starting and stopping with a backstitch. Press the seam allowances toward the orange rectangle, and then topstitch ¼" from the seam line as shown. Repeat the process to make a second piece for the clutch body.

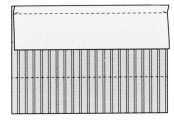

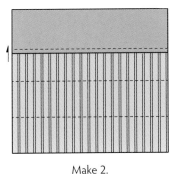

Make 2.

MAKING THE LINING

1. Follow the manufacturer's instructions to fuse the interfacing to the wrong side of the same-sized multicolored floral rectangles. Fuse the 2" x 4½" rectangle of interfacing to the orange 4" x 4½" rectangle, with the long edges aligned. (The interfacing will cover only half of the orange rectangle.)

2. To make the interior pocket, fold the prepared orange rectangle in half, right sides together, as shown. Pin the layers together. Starting and stopping with a backstitch, use a ¼" seam allowance to sew along the raw edges, leaving a 1" opening in the center of the bottom edge for turning. Clip the corners. Turn the piece right side out and gently push out the corners. Turn the open seam allowance under and press. The pocket should measure 1¾" x 4".

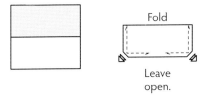

Fold

Leave open.

3. Topstitch ¼" from the top folded edge of the pocket, and then stitch ¼" below the first line of stitching.

4. Pin the pocket on the right side of a multicolored 6¾" x 10" rectangle, 2½" from the top edge and 3" in from the left side. Edgestitch around the side and bottom edges, starting and stopping with a backstitch.

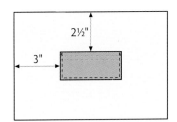

2½"

3"

5. Pin a multicolored 2¾" x 10" rectangle to the top of the piece from step 4, right sides together and raw edges aligned as shown. Using a ½" seam allowance, sew the pieces together, starting and stopping with a backstitch. Press the seam allowances open. Topstitch along each side of the seam using a ¼" seam allowance. Sew the remaining multicolored 6¾" x 10" and 2¾" x 10" rectangles together to make a second lining piece.

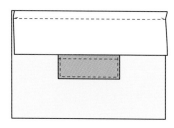

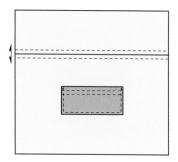

INSTALLING THE ZIPPER

1. To make a zipper tab, fold an orange 1½" x 2" rectangle in half lengthwise, wrong sides together. Open the strip and fold both raw edge to the center crease; press. Fold and press the strip in half lengthwise again. Repeat to make a second zipper tab.

2. Trim off the excess fabric at both zipper ends so that the zipper measures exactly 9".

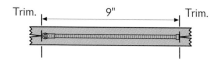

Trim. 9" Trim.

3. On the zipper-pull end, unzip the zipper slightly, and line up the teeth. Then insert the zipper into the tab; pin in place. Topstitch across the tab about ⅛" from the folded edge. Insert the other end of the zipper into the remaining tab. Pin and topstitch across the tab, being careful not to get your needle caught in the teeth of the zipper.

ASSEMBLING THE CLUTCH

1. Place a pleated piece on a flat surface, right side up, with the long edges at the top and bottom. With the zipper closed and right side facing down, place the zipper at the top of the pleated piece, aligning the top edges. The zipper pull should be on the left. Place a lining piece, wrong side up, on top of the zipper and the pleated piece, aligning the top edges. Pin the layers together along the top edge.

2. Using a zipper foot and a ¼" seam allowance, sew along the top edge. Flip the pieces open, wrong sides together as shown, and press. Using a walking foot, topstitch ¼" from the folded edge.

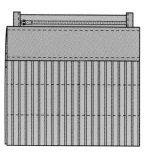

3. Repeat steps 1 and 2 to sew the remaining pleated and lining pieces on the opposite side of the zipper, making sure the sides are aligned with the previous half. The zipper pull will now be on the right.

4. Unzip the zipper halfway. You will be turning the clutch inside out through the open zipper, so don't forget this step!

5. Place the pleated pieces right sides together; pin along the raw edges. Repeat with the lining pieces. The zipper will be curving toward the pleated side. Stitch around the perimeter of the entire piece, leaving a 5" opening along the bottom edge of the lining. Clip the corners and turn the clutch right side out through the lining and open zipper. Gently push the corners out.

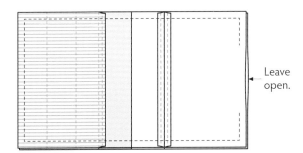

Leave open.

6. Topstitch the opening in the lining closed. Carrie likes to stitch along the entire bottom edge to camouflage the opening, making it look a bit more uniform. Tuck the lining into the clutch.

ASSEMBLING THE FLOWER

1. Use a compass to draw nine 2¾"-diameter circles on the wrong side of the teal print. Cut out the fabric circles on the drawn lines.

2. Layer two teal circles on top of each other, right sides up. Hand sew two or three stitches in the center to tack the circles together.

3. Fold a third circle in half, wrong sides together, and place it on top of the stack, aligning the raw edges. Tack the circle in place at the center. Repeat the process with another circle.

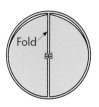

Fold

4. Fold a circle in half, wrong sides together, and then fold in half again. Place the quarter circle on top of the stack, aligning the raw edges. Tack in place at the center. Repeat the process to add three more quarter circles.

5. Fold the remaining circle in half, wrong sides together, and then in half two more times. Place the folded circle on top of the stack, with the point of the folds slightly off-center. Tack in place.

6. Fluff the fabric circles until the stack looks more like a flower. Carrie ran the flower under a water faucet for a few seconds, soaking the fabric. Then she tossed it in the dryer for about 10 minutes to fluff it and fray the edges.

7. Place the flower on the top-right corner of your clutch and hand sew in place, being careful to sew only through the top layer of the clutch. Stitch until the flower is secure.

Hand-Bound Journal

FINISHED SIZE: 7⅛" x 8¾"

Designed and made by Carrie Jung

Your beautiful thoughts should be kept in a beautiful journal.

MATERIALS

Yardage is based on 42"-wide fabric unless otherwise noted. Yields 1 journal.

2 squares, 12" x 12", of floral print for covers
1 skein of matching 6-strand embroidery floss
⅜ yard of 2"-wide grosgrain ribbon
32" x 40" sheet of book board for covers*
4 ounces of Sobo glue or craft glue*
½ cup of water
1½ teaspoons of methyl cellulose powder**
9.5-ounce resealable plastic container for mixing
    and storing glue
41 sheets, 8½" x 14", of 20 lb. copy paper
2 sheets, 8½" x 11", of 32 lb. paper or cardstock
Sharp X-Acto knife
Pencil
Foam brush
Paintbrush, ¼" wide
Waxed paper
Heavy weight or large heavy book for setting the book covers
Long straight pin

*Available at most craft stores
** Available at some art-supply stores and online

MIXING THE GLUE

In a resealable plastic container, mix the water and methyl cellulose powder. Seal the container and shake it vigorously for 30 seconds. Let the mixture sit for 24 hours. Then add the Sobo glue. Reseal the container and shake it vigorously.

MAKING THE BOOK COVERS

1. To make the book covers, use an X-Acto knife to cut two 7⅛" x 8¾" pieces of book board. The fewer cuts you make with the knife, the better; use a ruler to ensure a straight cut, and use a lot of downward pressure.

2. On one of the book covers, use a pencil to draw a line 1½" from one long edge. Then draw another line 1⅝" from the same edge. Measure 1" in from one of the short

edges and draw a line. On the same edge, measure 2⅝" in and draw a second line. In the same way, draw lines on the opposite short edge as shown.

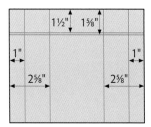

Draw lines.

3. Use an X-Acto knife to cut two ⅛" x 2⅝" slots as shown for binding the book. You may find it easier to cut the slots cleanly if you extend the cutting line about ⅛" beyond the edges.

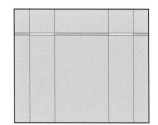

Cut out slots.

4. Repeat steps 2 and 3 to mark and cut slots in the second book cover.

5. It's important to label your boards so that the holes you've just cut will line up correctly when you sew the book together. (Theoretically, you shouldn't have to do this, but in reality this will help with alignment in the end.) On one of the covers, use a pencil to lightly label the marked side "outside" and the unmarked side "inside." On the second board, label the marked side "inside" and the unmarked side "outside."

6. Place one floral square wrong side up on a flat surface. Center one of the boards on the square, with the side marked "inside" facing up. Using a pencil, lightly trace the outline of the board to ensure the book cover is centered on the fabric.

7. Cut a square out of each corner of the fabric square, leaving about ¼" of fabric between the drawn corners and the cut corners. In the same way, mark and cut the second fabric square.

8. Using a foam brush, evenly coat the "outside" of one book cover with the glue mixture. Place the cover, glue side down, on the wrong side of the fabric square, aligning the edge of the cover with the marked lines. Flip the fabric and cover over, right side up, and use your hands to push out any air bubbles.

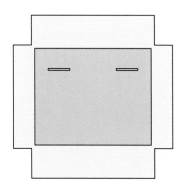

9. Turn the book cover over, with the fabric wrong side up. Paint a 1½"-wide strip of glue along the top and bottom edges of the book cover; add a little glue along the cut edge of the book cover. Smooth the fabric over the glue.

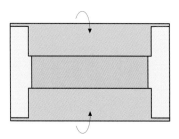

10. Paint glue along one end of the book cover in the same manner as before. Fold the fabric on both corners to hide the raw edges; then smooth the fabric over the glue as shown. Repeat the process on the other end of the book cover.

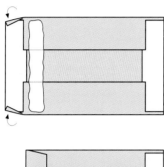

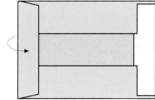

11. Repeat steps 8–10 to complete the second book cover.

12. Sandwich the book covers between two pieces of waxed paper and place them under a heavy weight or book overnight to dry.

PREPARING THE PAGES

1. Fold 40 sheets of 8½" x 14" copy paper in half so that the folded paper measures 8½" x 7". Arrange the paper into groups by placing four folded papers inside each other to create 10 booklets.

2. Fold the remaining sheet of copy paper in half. Using a pencil and ruler, boldly mark ¼", ⅞", 2½", 6", 7⅝", and 8¼" along the folded edge, starting from the bottom. Then refold the paper with the marks on the inside. Use a long straight pin to create a hole through each of the marks along the fold. It's very important that the hole is *exactly* on the fold and not off to one side. Placing a piece of cardboard

under the paper will make punching the holes easier. This paper is your hole-punching template.

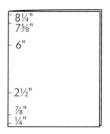

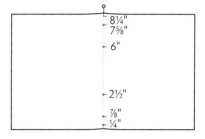

3. Place the template inside one of your booklet groups and align the sheets as evenly as possible. Push the pin through the booklet sheets using the template holes as your guide. Repeat for the remaining nine booklets.

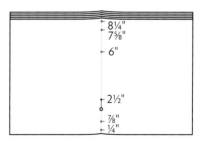

SEWING THE PAGES

1. Cut the grosgrain ribbon into two pieces, 6" long.

2. Using a 30" length of 6-strand embroidery floss, thread a needle and tie a double knot at one end. To sew the pages together, start on the outside of one booklet and insert the needle through the first punched hole (at the bottom edge) to the inside. Bring the needle to the outside through the second punched hole.

3. Insert the needle through the third hole, to the inside, and pull the thread taut. Insert a piece of ribbon between the thread and paper along the outside crease as shown. Bring the needle to the outside again through the fourth hole. Then insert the needle through the fifth hole, to the inside, and pull the thread taut. Insert the second piece of ribbon. Then bring the needle to the outside through the last hole. *Do not* cut the thread.

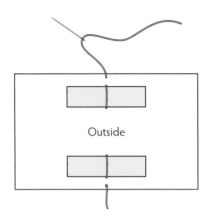

4. Repeat steps 2 and 3 to sew a second booklet to the first booklet, making sure to thread the ribbon between the paper and thread along the outside crease of the booklet. When you reach the last hole on the second booklet, tug lightly on the stitches to ensure there are no loose threads hiding anywhere. Then join the booklets by knotting the loose thread ends together, using the knot from the beginning as your anchor.

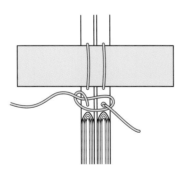

5. In the same way, sew a third booklet to the first two booklets. Tie a knot to secure it at the end by looping your needle through the thread from the previous booklet attachment.

Pull the thread almost taut, leaving a small ¼" loop. Then thread your needle through twice more and pull the thread taut to secure it.

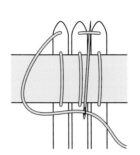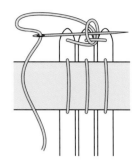

6. Continue stitching until all of the booklets are secured to each other. Cut your thread and center your pages on the ribbon. If you run out of thread, simply thread your needle and knot the new thread to the old. Just be sure the knot is located on the inside of one of the booklets, between two holes.

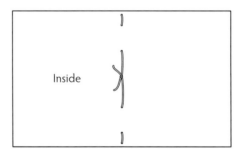

ASSEMBLING THE BOOK

1. After the book covers have dried overnight, remove them from the waxed paper. With an X-Acto knife, carefully cut slits in the fabric covering both slots on each cover.

2. Use the ¼"-wide paintbrush to apply the glue mixture to the holes, making sure to coat the raw edges. Once the glue is applied to all holes, tamp the loose fabric down so that it sticks to the edges. Then place the book covers back under the waxed paper and a heavy weight for another hour, or until the glue dries.

3. Once dry, if the fabric has pulled away from the sides of the holes, use the flat side of your X-Acto knife to tap it back into place. Then

This binding technique allows you to open your book to lie flat. As a journalist who takes a lot of notes, often without the support of a table, I appreciate this feature.
~ Carrie

insert one loose end of the booklet ribbon through the coordinating slot on one of the book covers going from the outside to the inside. Insert the second ribbon into the other hole on the same cover.

4. Pull the ribbons and align the book cover so that there is no space between the cover and the pages. Then generously apply glue under and over the loose ribbon on the inside of the cover. Cover the wet glue with waxed paper and a heavy weight; let dry for one hour. Repeat the process for the other book cover, making sure the ribbon is pulled taut before gluing it down.

5. Using the 32 lb. paper or cardstock, cut two 7" x 8½" sheets. Carefully apply glue to one side of one sheet, making sure to cover the corners and edges. Then, with the glue side down, center and place the paper on the inside of your book cover. Run your hands over the paper once or twice (especially the corners) to eliminate any air bubbles and to secure the paper to the cover. Repeat for the second cover.

6. Close the book without waxed paper and place it under a heavy weight overnight to dry.

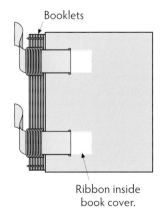

Ribbon inside book cover.

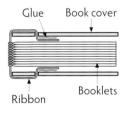

Top view

Big Bang Quilt

FINISHED QUILT SIZE: 72" x 84"
FINISHED BLOCK SIZE: 20" x 20"

Designed and made by Jessi Jung;
quilted by Judy Howard

Big-block quilts are making a huge comeback. They look beautiful on a bed, and they're so much fun to put together. This is Jessi's interpretation of a big-block quilt, made with two variations of the same block.

MATERIALS

Yardage is based on 42"-wide fabric unless otherwise noted.

4 yards of white fabric for block backgrounds, sashing, and border
¼ yard *each* of 5 fabric A prints for Star blocks (star and frame shape)
⅓ yard *each* of 5 fabric B prints for Star blocks (wreath shape)
⅓ yard *each* of 4 fabric C prints for Heart blocks (heart shape)
¼ yard *each* of 4 fabric D prints for Heart blocks (between heart shapes)
⅓ yard of fabric E for argyle diamonds
¼ yard of fabric F for argyle diamonds
⅝ yard of aqua fabric for binding
5¼ yards of fabric for backing
78" x 90" piece of batting

CUTTING

Referring to the Star block and Heart block diagrams on pages 39 and 41, plan your fabric selections for fabrics A–F before cutting.

From the white fabric, cut:
3 strips, 4½" x 42"; cut into 20 squares, 4½" x 4½"
15 strips, 2⅞" x 42"; cut into 188 squares, 2⅞" x 2⅞"
16 strips, 2½" x 42"; cut *12 of the strips* into:
    36 squares, 2½" x 2½"
    20 rectangles, 2½" x 4½"
    36 rectangles, 2½" x 6½"
1 strip, 20½" x 42"; cut into 12 strips, 2½" x 20½"
8 strips, 4¼" x 42"

From *each* fabric A print, cut:
4 squares, 2⅞" x 2⅞" (20 total)
1 square, 4½" x 4½" (5 total)
4 rectangles, 2½" x 4½" (20 total)
4 squares, 2½" x 2½" (20 total)

From *each* fabric B print, cut:
12 squares, 2⅞" x 2⅞" (60 total)
4 rectangles, 2½" x 8½" (20 total)
12 squares, 2½" x 2½" (60 total)

Continued on page 38

MAKING THE STAR BLOCKS

For ease of keeping all the fabrics in the block organized, instructions are for making one block at a time. After sewing each seam, press the seam allowances in the direction indicated by the arrows.

1. Referring to "Half-Square-Triangle Units" on page 7, use four white 2⅞" squares and four fabric A 2⅞" squares to make eight half-square-triangle units.

Make 8.

Continued from page 37

From *each* fabric C print, cut:
16 squares, 2⅞" x 2⅞" (64 total)
4 rectangles, 2½" x 8½" (16 total)
4 rectangles, 2½" x 4½" (16 total)

From *each* fabric D print, cut:
4 squares, 2⅞" x 2⅞" (16 total)
8 squares, 2½" x 2½" (32 total)

From fabric E, cut:
36 squares, 2⅞" x 2⅞"

From fabric F, cut:
24 squares, 2⅞" x 2⅞"

From the aqua fabric, cut:
9 strips, 2" x 42"

> ### Stretch Prevention
> Placing sandpaper under the squares helps prevent them from moving or stretching while you draw lines for the half-square-triangle units.

2. Sew two half-square-triangle units together as shown. Make a total of four units.

Make 4.

3. Lay out one fabric A 4½" square, four units from step 2, and four white 2½" squares as shown. Sew the pieces together in rows. Sew the rows together to complete the center unit.

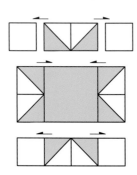
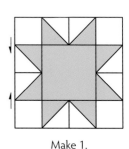

Make 1.

4. Repeat step 1 using 12 white 2⅞" squares and 12 fabric B 2⅞" squares to make 24 half-square-triangle units. Press the seam allowances toward fabric B.

5. Sew two half-square-triangle units together as shown. Make four units.

Make 4.

6. Sew two half-square-triangle units together as shown. Make eight units.

Make 8.

7. Lay out one unit from step 5, two units from step 6, one fabric B rectangle, and two fabric B 2½" squares as shown. Sew the pieces together in rows. Sew the rows together to complete a side unit. Make a total of four side units.

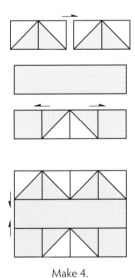

Make 4.

8. Lay out one fabric A 2½" square, one fabric B 2½" square, one white 2½" x 4½" rectangle, one fabric A 2½" x 4½" rectangle, and one white 2½" x 6½" rectangle as shown. Join the A and B squares. Add the A and white 4½"-long rectangles. Then add the white 6½"-long rectangle to complete the corner unit. Make two of each corner unit.

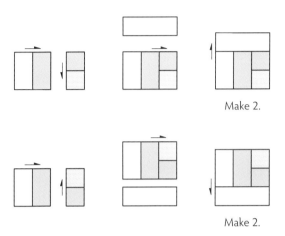

Make 2.

Make 2.

9. Lay out the center unit, the four side units, and the four corner units in three rows as shown. Sew the units together in rows and then join the rows to complete the block. The block should measure 20½" x 20½". Repeat to make a total of five Star blocks.

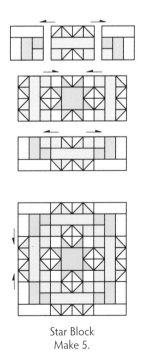

Star Block
Make 5.

Left: Star block;
right: Heart block

MAKING THE HEART BLOCKS

For ease of keeping all the fabrics in the block organized, instructions are for making one block at a time. After sewing each seam, press the seam allowances in the direction indicated by the arrows.

1. Referring to "Half-Square-Triangle Units," use 12 white 2⅞" squares and 12 fabric C 2⅞" squares to make 24 half-square-triangle units.

Make 24.

2. Sew two half-square-triangle units together as shown. Make a total of 12 units.

Make 12.

3. Lay out one white 4½" square, four units from step 2, and four fabric D 2½" squares as shown. Sew the pieces together in rows. Sew the rows together to complete the center unit.

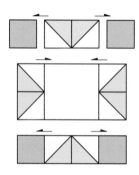
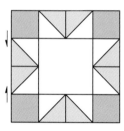

Make 1.

4. Repeat step 1 using four fabric C 2⅞" squares and four fabric D 2⅞" squares to make eight half-square-triangle units. Press the seam allowances toward fabric C.

5. Lay out two units from step 2, two units from step 4, one fabric C 2½" x 8½" rectangle, and one fabric C 2½" x 4½" rectangle as shown. Sew the pieces together in rows. Sew the rows together to make a side unit. Make four side units.

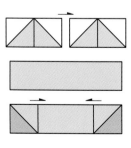
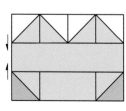

Make 4.

6. Lay out one white 2½" square, one fabric D 2½" square, one white 4½" square, and one white 2½" x 6½" rectangle as shown. Sew the 2½" squares together. Add the white 4½" square and then the white rectangle to make a corner unit. Make two of each corner unit.

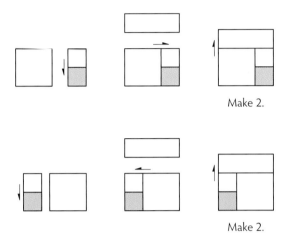

Make 2.

Make 2.

7. Lay out the center unit, the four side units, and the four corner units in three rows as shown. Sew the units together in rows and then join the rows to complete the block. The block should measure 20½" x 20½". Repeat to make a total of four Heart blocks.

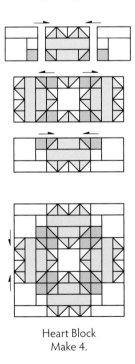

Heart Block
Make 4.

MAKING THE ARGYLE STRIPS

1. Use 36 white 2⅞" squares and 36 fabric E 2⅞" squares to make 72 half-square-triangle units. Press the seam allowances toward fabric E. In the same way, use 24 white 2⅞" squares and 24 fabric F 2⅞" squares to make 48 half-square-triangle units. Press the seam allowances toward fabric F.

Make
72.

Make
48.

2. Sew two matching units together as shown. Do not press the seam allowances at this time. Make the number of units indicated of each fabric combination.

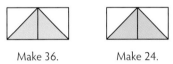

Make 36.

Make 24.

3. Lay out six fabric E units and four fabric F units in two rows as shown. Sew the units together in rows and press the seam allowances in opposite directions as indicated. Sew the two rows together and press the seam allowances in one direction. Make six argyle strips.

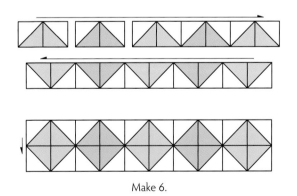

Make 6.

ASSEMBLING THE QUILT TOP

1. Referring to the quilt assembly diagram below, lay out the blocks, argyle strips, and white 2½" x 20½" strips in vertical rows as shown. Join the pieces in each row and press the seam allowances toward the sashing strips. The rows should measure 76½" long.

2. Referring to "Borders" on page 8, join the remaining white 2½"-wide strips end to end. From the pieced strip, cut two 76½"-long sashing strips. Sew the vertical rows and two sashing strips together, making sure to align the horizontal sashing strips. Press the seam allowances toward the sashing strips. The quilt center should measure 64½" x 76½".

3. Sew the white 4¼"-wide strips together end to end. From the pieced strip, cut two 76½"-long strips and sew them to opposite sides of the quilt top. Press the seam allowances toward the borders. From the remaining pieced strip, cut two 72"-long border strips and sew them to the top and bottom of the quilt top. Press the seam allowances toward the borders.

FINISHING

Refer to the sections "Backing" through "Binding" on pages 9–11 for help with the following finishing techniques as needed.

1. Cut and piece the backing fabric, and then layer the quilt top with batting and backing. Baste the layers together.

2. Quilt as desired.

3. Using the aqua 2"-wide strips, make and attach the binding.

Quilt assembly

Pencil Box Quilt

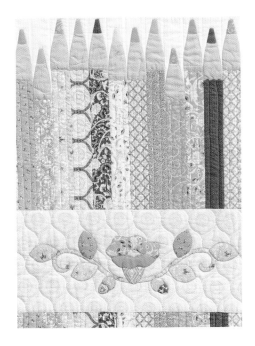

FINISHED QUILT SIZE: 48" x 53"

Designed and made by Jessi Jung;
quilted by Becky Putnam

Color your life with happiness . . . or at least color your quilting studio.

MATERIALS

Yardage is based on 42"-wide fabric unless otherwise noted.

1 Jelly Roll *OR* 40 strips, 2½" x 42", of assorted prints and
    solids for pencils, erasers, metal bands, lead points, and
    appliqué design*
1½ yards of aqua print for appliqué background, border,
    and binding
⅜ yard of brown solid for wooden ends of pencils
⅜ yard of white solid for background
3½ yards of fabric for backing
54" x 59" piece of batting
1⅓ yards of 22"-wide medium-weight fusible interfacing
1 yard of 16"-wide fusible web
1 yard of 20"-wide stabilizer
Monofilament and matching thread for appliqué

**Jessi used a fabric line that had 22 prints for the pencils, 2
coordinating prints for the erasers, 3 crosshatched prints for the
metal bands, and 5 solids for the lead points.*

CUTTING

*Choose fabrics for the eraser strips and metal strips before
choosing the fabrics for the pencils. Then select which pencil
fabrics you want to use for the longest (39½" long) pencils before
cutting. Set aside 4 or 5 solids to use for lead points and the
remaining strips for appliqués.*

From 2 prints for erasers, cut a *total* of:
22 squares, 2½" x 2½"

From 3 different prints for metal bands, cut a *total* of:
22 rectangles, 2½" x 3½"

From the pencil fabrics, cut a *total* of:
13 strips, 2½" x 39½"
6 strips, 2½" x 38½"
3 strips, 2½" x 36½"

From the white solid, cut:
13 rectangles, 2½" x 5½"
6 rectangles, 2½" x 6½"
3 rectangles, 2½" x 8½"

Continued on page 45

Continued on page 43

From the aqua print, cut:
2 strips, 10½" x 42"
6 strips, 2¼" x 42"
6 strips, 2" x 42"

From the stabilizer, cut:
22 rectangles, 3" x 10"

From the interfacing, cut:
1 strip, 10½" x 44½"

MAKING THE PENCILS

Referring to the photo on page 44 and the quilt assembly diagram on page 47 for placement guidance, arrange the pencil pieces on a design wall, alternating the colors of eraser squares and the colors of metal-band rectangles as shown.

1. Sew an eraser 2½" square to a metal band 2½" x 3½" rectangle. Make 22.

Make 22.

2. Sew a white 2½" x 5½" rectangle to each pencil 39½"-long strip to make 13 strips. Sew a white 2½" x 6½" rectangle to each pencil 38½"-long strip to make six strips. Sew a white 2½" x 8½" rectangle to each pencil 36½"-long strip to make three strips. Each strip should measure 44½" long.

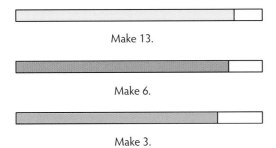

Make 13.

Make 6.

Make 3.

3. Sew a unit from step 1 to the pencil end of each 44½"-long strip to make 22 pencils.

Press all seam allowances in one direction, alternating the direction from one pencil to the next.

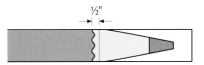

Make 22 pencils.

4. Referring to "Machine Appliqué" on page 7 and using the pencil patterns on page 48, prepare the shapes for fusible appliqué. Referring to the photo and using the appropriate fabrics, cut out each shape. Layer the shapes in numerical order on the pencil strips from step 3, overlapping the wood atop the pencil by about ½", and fuse in place.

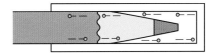

Take a Stand

If your machine holds spools horizontally, place monofilament on a thread stand separate from your machine. When positioned vertically, the thread will feed off the spool better and be less likely to break or stretch.

5. Center and pin a piece of stabilizer underneath each appliqué shape. Stitch around each shape using a zigzag stitch and monofilament. Gently remove the stabilizer.

6. Lay out the pencils as shown in the quilt assembly diagram on page 47. Sew the pencils together. Press the seam allowances in one direction.

MAKING THE APPLIQUÉD STRIP

1. Join the aqua 10½"-wide strips end to end. From the pieced strip, cut one 44½"-long strip. Follow the manufacturer's instructions to fuse the interfacing to the wrong side of the aqua strip.

2. Fold the aqua strip in half lengthwise, wrong sides together; then fold it in half crosswise. Lightly press the folds to establish centering guidelines.

3. Referring to "Machine Appliqué" and using the flower, leaf, and vine patterns on page 48, prepare the shapes for fusible appliqué. Referring to the quilt photo and using the appropriate fabrics, cut out each shape. Layer the shapes on the aqua strip in numerical order using the centering lines, again referring to the project photo and also to the appliqué placement diagram below for guidance. Fuse and stitch around each shape using a blanket stitch and matching thread.

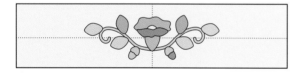

Appliqué placement

4. Turn the top and bottom edges of the aqua strip under ¼" and press. Center the strip across the pencils and pin in place. Topstitch across the top and bottom edges of the aqua strip. Trim the side edges even with the sides of the quilt top.

ADDING THE BORDER

Jessi added borders with mitered corners to this quilt to create a box appearance.

1. Join the aqua 2¼"-wide strips end to end. From the pieced strip, cut four 55"-long strips. Fold each strip in half crosswise and finger-press the fold to crease it.

2. Fold the quilt top in half along one edge and finger-press the fold to crease it. With right sides together, match the crease mark of an aqua strip to the crease mark on the quilt top. Sew the strip to the quilt top, beginning and ending ¼" from the raw edge of the quilt top with a backstitch. Press the seam allowances toward the border. Repeat to sew a border strip to the opposite side of the quilt top.

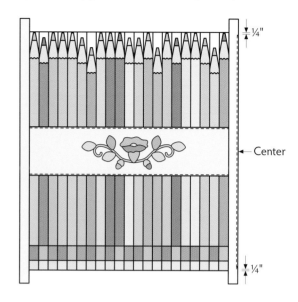

3. Repeat step 2 to sew the remaining strips to the top and bottom of the quilt top.

4. Working with one corner at a time, fold the quilt top diagonally, right sides together. Line up the edges of the border strips and pin them together as shown. Using a pencil, draw a 45° angle on the wrong side of the strip, starting at the intersection of the seam lines as shown. Sew along the marked line, backstitching at both ends.

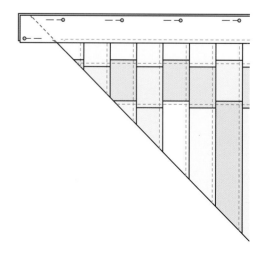

5. Remove the pins. Trim the seam allowances to ¼" and then press them open. Miter the remaining corners in the same manner.

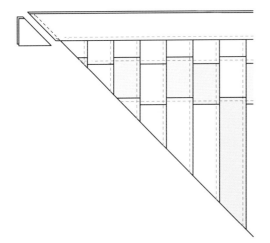

FINISHING

Refer to the sections "Backing" through "Binding" on pages 9–11 for help with the following finishing techniques as needed.

1. Cut and piece the backing fabric, and then layer the quilt top with batting and backing. Baste the layers together.
2. Quilt as desired.
3. Using the aqua 2"-wide strips, make and attach the binding.

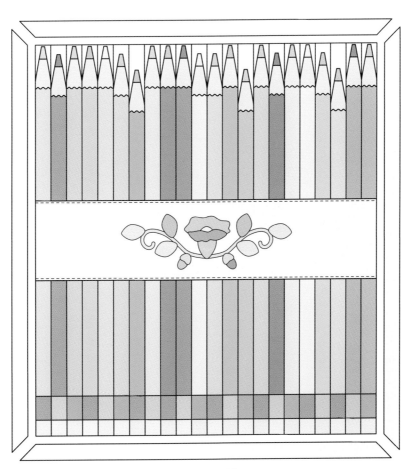

Quilt assembly

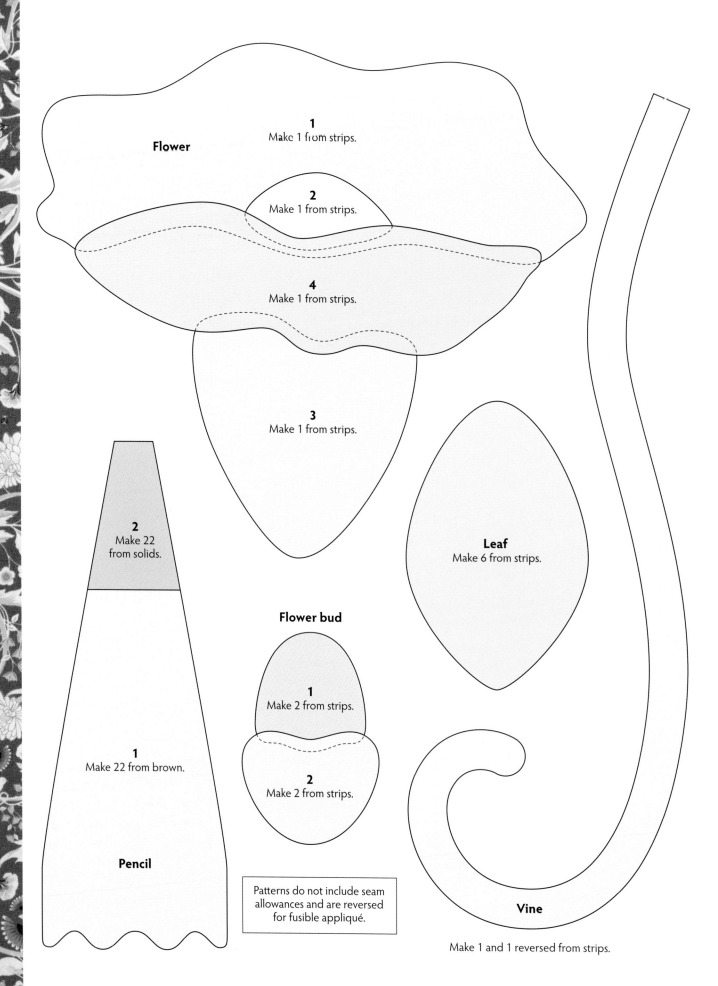

Flower

1
Make 1 from strips.

2
Make 1 from strips.

4
Make 1 from strips.

3
Make 1 from strips.

2
Make 22 from solids.

1
Make 22 from brown.

Pencil

Flower bud

1
Make 2 from strips.

2
Make 2 from strips.

Leaf
Make 6 from strips.

Vine

Make 1 and 1 reversed from strips.

Patterns do not include seam allowances and are reversed for fusible appliqué.

Curling Iron Cozy

FINISHED SIZE: 10" x 13" (overall size)

Designed and made by Carrie Jung

Create a cozy spot for your hot curling iron or flat iron. Just toss the styling tool in here and get on with your day—no need to wait for it to cool first.

MATERIALS

Yardage is based on 42"-wide fabric unless otherwise noted.

¼ yard of fabric A for outer cozy and small-pocket lining

½ yard of fabric B for outer cozy, lining, large pocket, and small pocket

¼ yard of fabric C for facing and binding

⅜ yard of insulated batting

⅛ yard of 22"-wide medium-weight fusible interfacing

CUTTING

From fabric A, cut:

2 rectangles, 4¼" x 10"

1 rectangle, 3" x 13"

From fabric B, cut:

1 rectangle, 5½" x 10"

1 rectangle, 10" x 13"

2 rectangles, 5½" x 11¾"

1 rectangle, 3" x 13"

From fabric C, cut:

1 rectangle, 1¾" x 12"

2 strips, 2" x 42"

From the fusible interfacing, cut:

1 rectangle, 3" x 13"

From the insulated batting, cut:

1 rectangle, 10" x 13"

1 rectangle, 5½" x 11¾"

ASSEMBLING THE COZY

1. Sew the fabric A 4¼" x 10" rectangles to opposite sides of the fabric B 5½" x 10" rectangle, right sides together. Press the seam allowances open.

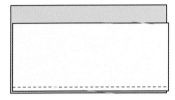

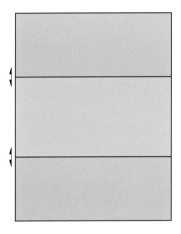

2. Create a "quilt sandwich" by placing the pieced rectangle from step 1 wrong side up on a flat surface. Place the batting 10" x 13" rectangle over the pieced rectangle. Center the fabric B 10" x 13" rectangle over the batting, right side up. Align the edges and pin the layers together. Quilt as desired to complete the main panel.

3. To make the large pocket panel, place one fabric B 5½" x 11¾" rectangle wrong side up on a flat surface. Place the batting 5½" x 11¾" rectangle over the pieced rectangle. Center the second fabric B 5½" x 11¾" rectangle over the batting, right side up. Align the edges and pin the layers together. Quilt as desired.

Trim It Up

If the fabric shifts during the quilting process and your panels look a little wonky, don't panic. Just use your rotary cutter and ruler to clean up the edges.

4. Referring to "Binding" on page 10, use one fabric C 2"-wide strip to make binding. Bind the top short end of the large pocket panel.

5. On the short end of the fabric C 1¾"-wide strip, fold over ¼" to the wrong side and press. Press the strip in half lengthwise, wrong sides together.

6. Align the large pocket panel with the bottom-right corner of the main panel. Align the edges of the folded strip from step 5 with the left edge of the large pocket, aligning the raw edges as shown. Pin and sew along the raw edges, beginning and ending at the edges of the main panel as shown. (This will give the seam lines of the cozy a uniform look from the outside.)

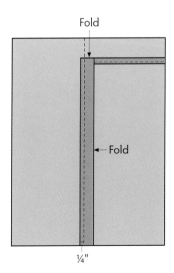

Fold

Fold

¼"

7. Flip the fabric C strip to the left and topstitch along the folded edge, sewing from raw edge to raw edge of the main panel as shown.

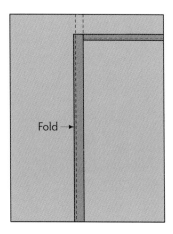

Fold →

8. Flip the large pocket to the opposite end of the main panel, align the raw edge, and baste in place along the sides.

9. Following the manufacturer's instructions, fuse the interfacing to the wrong side of the fabric B 3" x 13" rectangle. Pin and sew the interfaced rectangle to one long edge of the fabric A 3" x 13" rectangle, right sides together. Fold the rectangles, wrong sides together, and press. Sew a decorative stitch ¼" from the folded edge to make the small pocket.

10. With the fabric B rectangle on top, baste the small pocket to the main panel as shown.

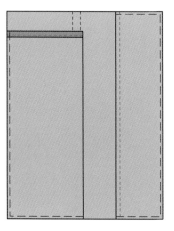

11. Using the remaining fabric C binding strip, bind the raw edges of the cozy.

Fly-Away Canvases: Andy Warhol-Style

FINISHED SIZE: 10" x 8" each

Designed and made by Jessi Jung

Jessi has always been a huge fan of Andy Warhol's screen prints. He's most famous for his Campbell's Soup prints and the Marilyn Monroe series. These canvases are her tribute to Warhol's style and use of color.

MATERIALS

Yardage is based on 42"-wide fabric unless otherwise noted. Yields 3 canvases.

3 rectangles, 12" x 14", of assorted prints for backgrounds
12 scraps, 3" x 10", of assorted prints for body and wing appliqués
3 scraps, 4" x 4", of assorted prints for leg appliqués
½ yard of 16"-wide fusible web
3 prestretched artist's canvases, 8" x 10"
Staple gun and staples
Monofilament for appliqué
3 pieces, 8" x 10", of stabilizer

ASSEMBLING THE CANVAS

Instructions are for making one canvas. If you're making the entire set, Jessi recommends selecting the fabrics for each canvas before starting. When creating appliqué designs that use five different fabrics, such as these, it's best to choose fabric groups that contain similar color palettes.

1. Fold an assorted print 12" x 14" rectangle in half in both directions, wrong sides together, and lightly press to mark the center.
2. Referring to "Machine Appliqué" on page 7 and using the pattern on page 56, prepare the shapes for fusible appliqué. Referring to the photo on page 54 and using the assorted scraps, cut out one of each shape.

3. Layer the shapes in numerical order in the center of the rectangle and fuse in place. Center and pin a piece of stabilizer to the back of the rectangle. Stitch around each shape using a zigzag stitch and monofilament. Gently remove the stabilizer.

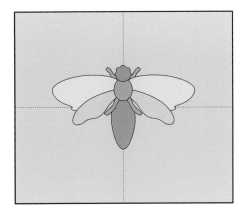

4. Place the appliquéd rectangle right side down on a flat surface and center an 8" x 10" canvas on top of the rectangle. On one long side, fold the rectangle over the wood frame. Using a staple gun, staple the fabric to the wood frame by placing one staple in the center. Spin the canvas around to the opposite side. Pull the fabric taut over the wood frame and place one staple in the center of the second side.

5. Rotate the canvas 90°. Pull the fabric taut and place one staple in the center of the third side. Then rotate the canvas, pull the fabric taut, and place one staple in the center of the last side.

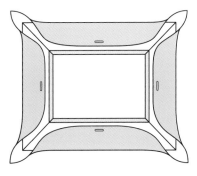

6. Working from the center toward each corner, pull the fabric taut and staple along each side, placing the staples 1" to 2" apart. Fold the excess fabric in the corners and staple it in place.

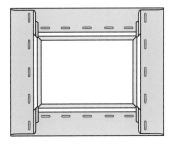

7. Repeat steps 1–6 to make a total of three canvases.

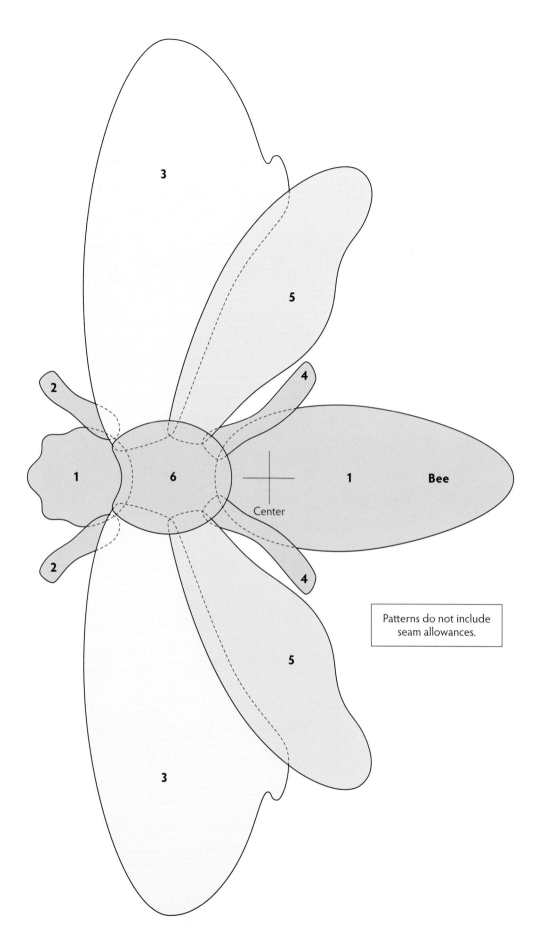

3

2

5

4

2

1

6

1

Bee

Center

4

5

3

Patterns do not include
seam allowances.

He Loves Me Daisy Quilt

FINISHED QUILT SIZE: 58" x 58"
FINISHED BLOCK SIZE: 10" x 10"

Designed and made by Jessi Jung; quilted by Judy Howard

He loves me . . . He loves me not . . . He loves me!

MATERIALS

Yardage is based on 42"-wide fabric unless otherwise noted.

1¾ yards of light-blue print for block backgrounds and outer border
1¼ yards of white solid for setting squares and triangles
⅞ yard of light-green print for blocks and inner border
⅝ yard of red print for blocks, inner-border corner squares, and binding
1 charm pack *OR* 42 squares, 5" x 5", of assorted prints for flower and leaf appliqués
10" x 10" square of brown print for stem appliqués
3¾ yards of fabric for backing
64" x 64" piece of batting
1¾ yards of 16"-wide fusible web
1½ yards of 20"-wide stabilizer
Monofilament and blue thread for appliqué

CUTTING

From the light-blue print, cut:
9 squares, 7½" x 7½"
4 squares, 6½" x 6½"
5 strips, 6½" x 42"

From the light-green print, cut:
13 strips, 2" x 42"; cut *8 of the strips* into 36 rectangles, 2" x 7½"

From the red print, cut:
9 strips, 2" x 42"; cut *2 of the strips* into 40 squares, 2" x 2"

From the white solid, cut:
4 squares, 10½" x 10½"
2 squares, 15½" x 15½"; cut the squares into quarters diagonally to yield 8 side triangles
2 squares, 8" x 8"; cut the squares in half diagonally to yield 4 corner triangles

From the stabilizer, cut:
9 squares, 7½" x 7½"
4 squares, 6½" x 6½"

MAKING THE BLOCKS

1. Referring to "Machine Appliqué" on page 7 and using the patterns on page 61, prepare the shapes for fusible appliqué. Referring to the photo on page 58 and using 35 of the print 5" squares, cut out the petals. Use the remaining 5" squares to cut out the flower tops. Use the brown 10" square to cut out the stems.

2. Fold each light-blue 7½" square in half diagonally and lightly crease to establish a centering line. Position two leaves in one corner of a light-blue square, aligning the side edges with the edge of the square and overlapping the leaves as shown. Center a stem on the creased line, atop the leaves. Trim any edges that extend beyond the edge of the square or protrude from underneath the stem. Fuse the shapes in place. Repeat to make nine blocks.

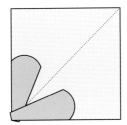

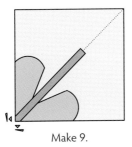

Make 9.

3. In the opposite corner of a light-blue square from step 2, position two petals on each side of the center line, making sure the side edges butt against each other. Add a flower top in the corner, aligning the edges of the

flower top with the corner of the light-blue square and overlapping the base of the petals about ¼". Adjust the position of the petals, if needed. Fuse the shapes in place. Repeat to make nine blocks.

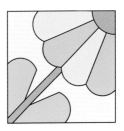

Make 9.

4. Center and pin a 7½" piece of stabilizer to the back of each square.

5. Using a zigzag stitch and monofilament, stitch between the petals only. Then thread your machine with blue thread and stitch around each shape using a blanket stitch. Make nine blocks. Gently remove the stabilizer.

Make 9.

6. Repeat steps 2–5 using the light-blue 6½" squares to make four corner blocks as shown. Set the blocks aside until quilt assembly.

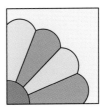

Make 4.

7. Sew light-green rectangles to opposite sides of a block from step 5. Press the seam allowances toward the rectangles. Sew a red square to each end of two additional light-green rectangles. Press the seam allowances toward the light-green rectangles, and then sew the pieced strips to the top and bottom of the block as shown. Press the seam allowances toward the pieced strips. Make nine blocks.

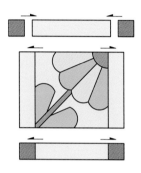
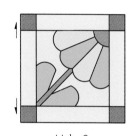

Make 9.

ASSEMBLING THE QUILT TOP

1. Arrange the blocks, the white squares, and the white side and corner triangles in diagonal rows. Sew the blocks, squares, and side triangles together into rows. Press the seam allowances toward the white squares and triangles.

2. Sew the rows together, matching the seam intersections. Add the corner triangles last. Trim and square up the quilt top, making sure to leave ¼" beyond the points of all the blocks for seam allowance. The quilt top should measure 43" x 43".

3. Join the remaining light-green 2"-wide strips end to end. From the pieced strip, cut four 43"-long strips. Sew light-green strips to opposite sides of the quilt top. Press the seam allowances toward the strips.

4. Sew a red square to each end of the two remaining light-green strips. Press the seam allowances toward the light-green strips, and then sew the strips to the top and bottom of the quilt top to complete the inner border. Press the seam allowances toward the light-green strips.

5. Join the light-blue 6½"-wide strips end to end. From the pieced strip, cut four 46"-long strips. Sew light-blue strips to opposite sides of the quilt top. Press the seam allowances toward the light-blue strips.

6. Sew a corner block to each end of the two remaining light-blue strips as shown in the quilt assembly diagram below. Press the seam allowances toward the light-blue strips, and then sew the strips to the top and bottom of the quilt to complete the outer border. Press the seam allowances toward the light-blue strips.

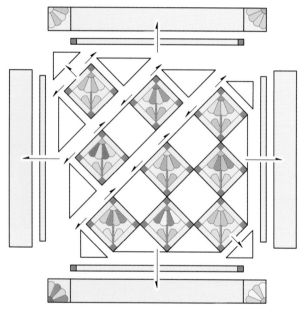

Quilt assembly

FINISHING

Refer to the sections "Backing" through "Binding" on pages 9–11 for help with the following finishing techniques as needed.

1. Cut and piece the backing fabric, and then layer the quilt top with batting and backing. Baste the layers together.

2. Quilt as desired.

3. Using the red 2"-wide strips, make and attach the binding.

About the Quilting

Jessi's quilter, Judy Howard, had a lot of fun quilting this project. Thanks to the simple pattern and the selection of solid fabric for the back of the quilt, the artistry of her stitches can really shine. If you're not quite as confident in your quilting prowess, using a busy print for the backing will help disguise your quilting.

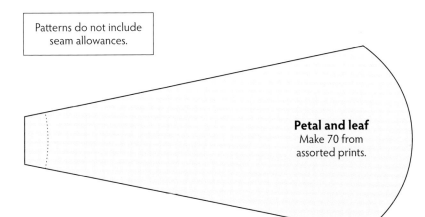

Patterns do not include seam allowances.

Flower top
Make 13 from assorted prints.

Petal and leaf
Make 70 from assorted prints.

Stem
Make 9 from brown print.

Makeup Bag

FINISHED SIZE: 9" x 7¾"

Designed and made by Carrie Jung

We have a soft spot for hummingbirds in this family. Carrie thinks the bird motif adds a little something extra to this basic bag pattern. However, if you can't bear to cover up your fabric, you can skip the appliqué step altogether and let your fabric do the talking.

MATERIALS

Yardage is based on 42"-wide fabric unless otherwise noted. Yields 1 bag.

⅓ yard of blue print for outer bag
⅓ yard of fabric for lining
6" x 6" square of green print for appliqué
½ yard of 22"-wide medium-weight fusible interfacing
6" x 6" square of fusible web
6" x 6" square of stabilizer
10" zipper to match outer fabric
6" length of coordinating ribbon for embellishment

CUTTING

From the blue print, cut:
2 rectangles, 7½" x 9½"

From the lining fabric, cut:
2 rectangles, 7½" x 9½"

From the interfacing, cut:
4 rectangles, 7½" x 9½"

MAKING THE BAG

1. Follow the manufacturer's instructions to fuse the interfacing to wrong side of the blue rectangles and the lining rectangles.
2. Referring to "Machine Appliqué" on page 7 and using the pattern on page 65, prepare the hummingbird for fusible appliqué. Using the green square, cut out the hummingbird shape.

3. Center the hummingbird along the blue rectangle, keeping in mind that about 2" of the bottom will be folded under in a later step. Fuse in place. Center and pin the square of stabilizer to the back of the rectangle. Stitch around the shape using a blanket stitch. Gently remove the stabilizer.

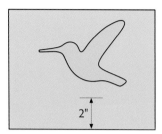

2"

4. Place a lining piece on a flat surface, right side up, with the long edges at the top and bottom. With the zipper closed and right side up, place the zipper at the top of the lining piece, aligning the top edges. Place a blue rectangle, wrong side up, over the zipper and lining, aligning the top edges. Pin the layers together along the top edge.

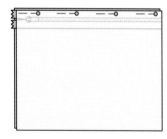

5. Using a zipper foot and starting and stopping with a backstitch, sew along the top edge of the zipper, as close to the teeth as possible. Press the blue rectangle and the lining rectangle away from the zipper. Place the rectangles wrong sides together and use a walking foot to topstitch ¼" from the seam.

6. Repeat steps 4 and 5 to add the remaining blue rectangle and lining rectangle on the opposite side of the zipper, making sure the side edges of the rectangles are aligned with the previous half.

7. Unzip the zipper about halfway. You'll be turning the bag inside out through the open zipper, so you don't want to forget this step!

8. Bring the blue rectangles right sides together; pin along the raw edges. Repeat with the lining rectangles. Make sure the zipper is curving toward the blue rectangles.

9. Sew around the perimeter of the entire piece, using a ½" seam allowance and leaving a 4" opening along the bottom edge of the lining.

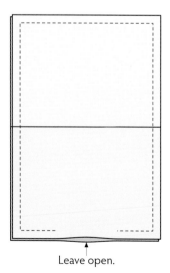

Leave open.

FINISHING THE BAG

1. To form the bottom corners, fold the lining right sides together, aligning a side seam on the bottom seam, and pin. Measure 1½" from the corner and draw a line perpendicular to the seam. Sew along this line. Trim ¼" from the stitching line. Repeat to box the other corner. Press.

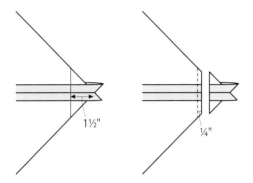

1½"

¼"

2. Repeat step 1 to box the corners on the outer bag.

3. Turn the bag right side out through the lining and open zipper and push the corners out.

4. Topstitch the opening in the lining closed. Carrie likes to stitch along the entire bottom edge to camouflage the opening, making it look a bit more uniform. Tuck the lining into the bag. Tie the ribbon to the zipper pull.

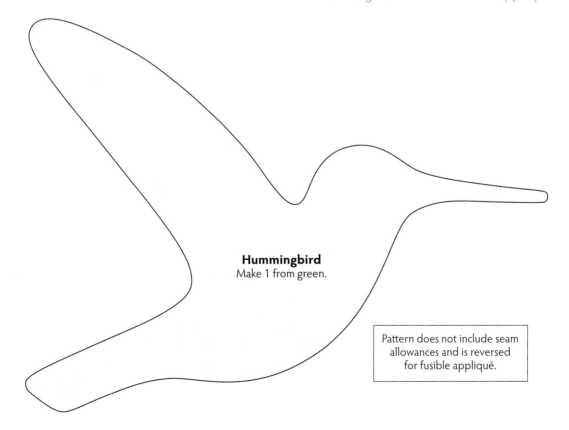

Hummingbird
Make 1 from green.

Pattern does not include seam allowances and is reversed for fusible appliqué.

Celebrations Quilt

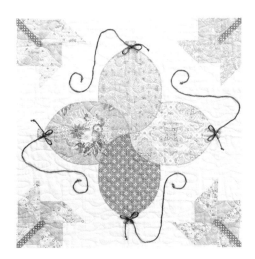

FINISHED QUILT SIZE: 46" x 46"
FINISHED BLOCK SIZE: 8" x 8"

Designed and pieced by Jessi Jung; quilted by Becky Putnam

This wall hanging makes a perfect backdrop for a child's birthday party, or use it as a festive covering for the gift table.

MATERIALS

Yardage is based on 42"-wide fabric unless otherwise noted.

1⅞ yards of white solid for background and candy apple appliqués
⅝ yard of aqua floral for outer border
½ yard of red print for pinwheel sticks and binding
⅜ yard of yellow solid for snow cone appliqués and accent border
1 square, 10" x 10", *each* of blue floral, yellow floral, pink floral, and green floral for pinwheels
1 square, 10" x 10", *each* of blue, green, red, and yellow prints for balloon appliqués
1 square, 10" x 10", of dark-green solid for spoon appliqués
1 square, 10" x 10", of red solid for candy apple appliqués
12 squares, 5" x 5", of assorted prints for snow cone and star appliqués
1 square, 5" x 5", of light-green print for candy apple sticks
⅛ yard of teal print for pinwheels
3 yards of fabric for backing
52" x 52" piece of batting
1⅔ yards of 16"-wide fusible web
2½ yards of 20"-wide stabilizer
2⅔ yards of red satin cording for balloons
Blue thread for appliqué

CUTTING

From the white solid, cut:
6 strips, 8½" x 42"; cut into 21 squares, 8½" x 8½"
2 strips, 2½" x 42"; cut into 32 squares, 2½" x 2½"
8 squares, 2⅞" x 2⅞"

From the teal print, cut:
8 squares, 2⅞" x 2⅞"

From *each* of the blue, yellow, pink, and green floral squares, cut:
4 squares, 2⅞" x 2⅞" (16 total)

From the yellow solid, cut
4 strips, 1" x 40½"

Continued on page 68

Continued on page 67

From the aqua floral, cut:
2 strips, 3¼" x 40½"
3 strips, 3¼" x 42"

From the red print, cut:
5 strips, 2" x 42"

From the stabilizer, cut:
1 square, 20" x 20"
16 squares, 8½" x 8½"
4 rectangles, 1" x 12"

MAKING THE PINWHEEL BLOCKS

1. Referring to "Half-Square-Triangle Units" on page 7, sew a teal square to a blue floral square to make two half-square-triangle units. Press the seam allowances toward the teal triangle. Make a total of four blue units.

Make 4.

2. Repeat step 1 to make four half-square-triangle units using two teal squares and two yellow floral squares, four units using two teal squares and two pink floral squares, and four units using two teal squares and two green floral squares.

Make 4 of each.

3. Sew a white 2⅞" square to each remaining blue, yellow, pink, and green floral square to make half-square-triangle units. Press the seam allowances toward the floral squares. Make four units of *each* color.

Make 4 of each.

4. Arrange the blue-and-teal units from step 1, the blue floral units from step 3, and eight white 2½" squares in four rows to form a pinwheel as shown. Sew the pieces together in rows. Press the seam allowances in opposite directions from row to row. Sew the rows together and press the seam allowances in one direction.

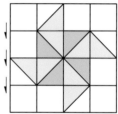
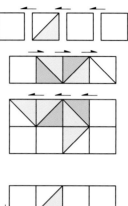

5. Repeat step 4 to make one Pinwheel block using the yellow floral units, one Pinwheel block using the pink floral units, and one Pinwheel block using the green floral units.

MAKING THE APPLIQUÉ BLOCKS

1. Referring to "Machine Appliqué" on page 7 and using the patterns on pages 72–74, prepare the shapes for fusible appliqué. Referring to the photo on page 66 and using the appropriate prints, cut out each shape. Set aside the balloon and pinwheel stick shapes to fuse during quilt assembly.

2. Sew two white 8½" squares together and press the seam allowances open. Make four two-square blocks. Fold each block in half lengthwise and lightly crease to mark a center line. Layer a candy apple, stick, and highlight shape in numerical order on each block, centering the shapes on the creased line and

placing them 2½" from the bottom edge as shown. Fuse the shapes in place. Make a total of four candy apple blocks.

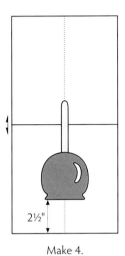

2½"

Make 4.

3. Fold 12 white 8½" squares in half in both directions and lightly crease to establish centering lines.

4. Fuse a star shape to one corner of a white square. Make a total of four star blocks.

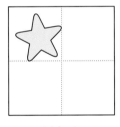

Make 4.

5. Layer snow cone shapes in numerical order in the center of a white square and fuse in place. Make a total of eight snow cone blocks, making sure to position four spoons on the right side of the cone and four spoons on the left side of the cone.

Make 4 of each.

6. Center and pin an 8½" square of stabilizer to the back of each block, under the appliqué shape. Stitch around each shape using a blanket stitch and blue thread. Gently remove the stabilizer.

ASSEMBLING THE QUILT TOP

1. Arrange one star block, one snow cone block with the spoon on the right, one snow cone block with the spoon on the left, and one Pinwheel block as shown. Sew the blocks into rows. Press the seam allowances toward the snow cone blocks. Join the rows and press the seam allowances toward the star block. Make four of these blocks.

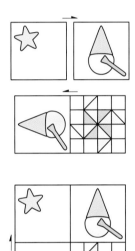

Make 4.

2. Fuse a red pinwheel stick to each block from step 1, referring to the photo for placement guidance. Pin a 1" x 12" rectangle of stabilizer under each pinwheel-stick appliqué. Stitch around each pinwheel stick using a blanket stitch and blue thread. Gently remove the stabilizer.

3. Arrange the blocks from step 2, the candy apple blocks, and the remaining white 8½" square in three rows as shown. Sew the pieces into rows. Press the seam allowances toward the candy apple blocks. Sew the rows together and press the seam allowances toward the center row. The quilt top should measure 40½" x 40½".

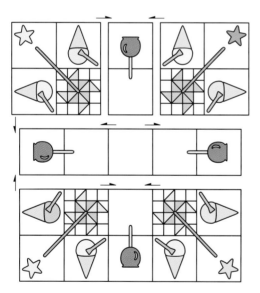

4. Fold each balloon shape in half vertically, wrong sides together, and finger-press the fold to mark a center line. *Do not use an iron.* Fold the quilt top in half in both directions and finger-press to establish centering lines. Place the balloons in the center of the quilt top, using the creased lines as guides and overlapping the balloons as shown in the photo (page 66). Fuse the balloons in place.

5. Pin the 20" square of stabilizer under the appliqué shape. Stitch around each balloon using a blanket stitch and blue thread. Gently remove the stabilizer.

6. Press each yellow 1"-wide strip in half lengthwise, wrong sides together. Align the raw edges of the folded strips with the side edges of the quilt top. Machine baste the strips using a scant ¼" seam allowance. Align the raw edges of the remaining folded strips with the top and bottom edges of the quilt top, raw edges aligned and overlapping the strips in the corners. Machine baste in place.

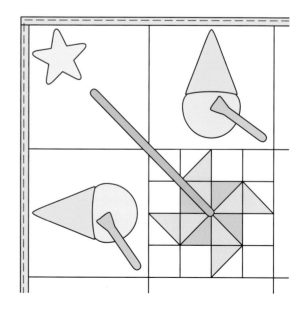

Border Accent

A flat, narrow border adds a little something extra, giving the quilt an extra layer of interest and a splash of color.

7. Sew the aqua floral 3¼" x 40½" strips to opposite sides of the quilt top. Press the seam allowances toward the borders. Join the 3¼" x 42" strips end to end. From the pieced strip cut two 46"-long strips and sew them to the top and bottom of the quilt. Press the seam allowances toward the border.

FINISHING

Refer to the sections "Backing" through "Binding" on pages 9–11 for help with the following finishing techniques as needed.

1. Cut and piece the backing fabric, and then layer the quilt top with batting and backing. Baste the layers together.
2. Quilt as desired.
3. Using the red 2"-wide strips, make and attach the binding.
4. Cut the red cording into four 24" lengths to make balloon strings. Knot both ends of each string to stop any unraveling. Tie a bow on one end of each string. Pin a string to each balloon, referring to the photo for placement guidance. Hand tack each string to the quilt, being careful to sew through the quilt top and batting only.

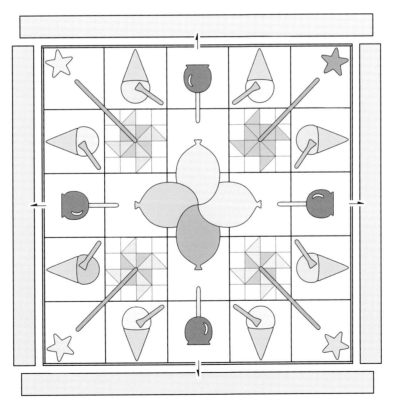

Quilt assembly

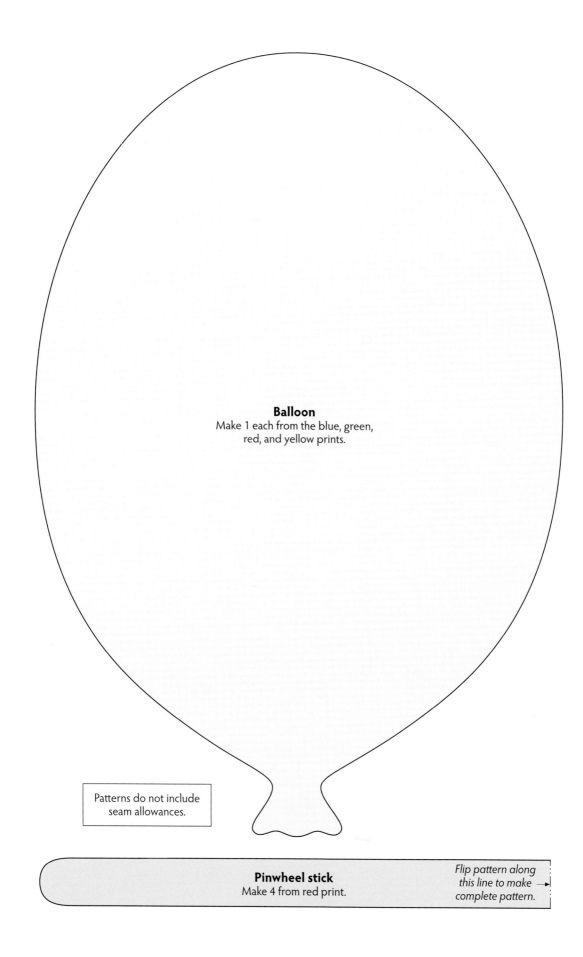

Balloon
Make 1 each from the blue, green,
red, and yellow prints.

Patterns do not include
seam allowances.

Pinwheel stick
Make 4 from red print.

*Flip pattern along
this line to make
complete pattern.*

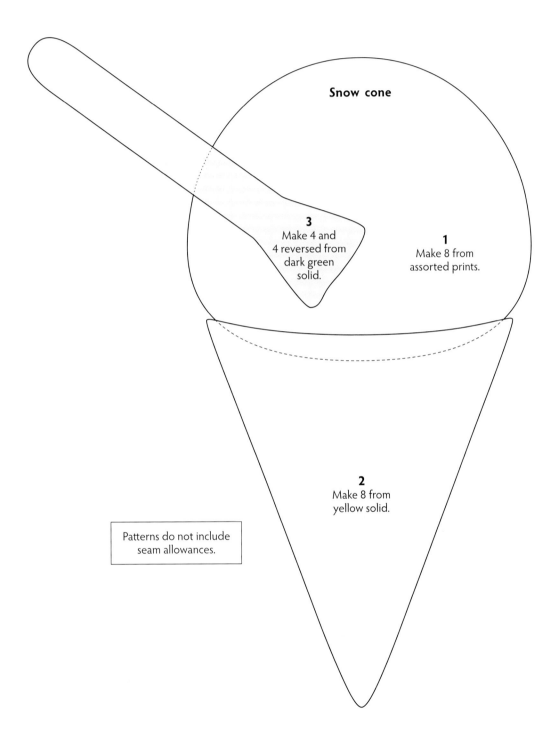

Snow cone

3
Make 4 and
4 reversed from
dark green
solid.

1
Make 8 from
assorted prints.

2
Make 8 from
yellow solid.

Patterns do not include
seam allowances.

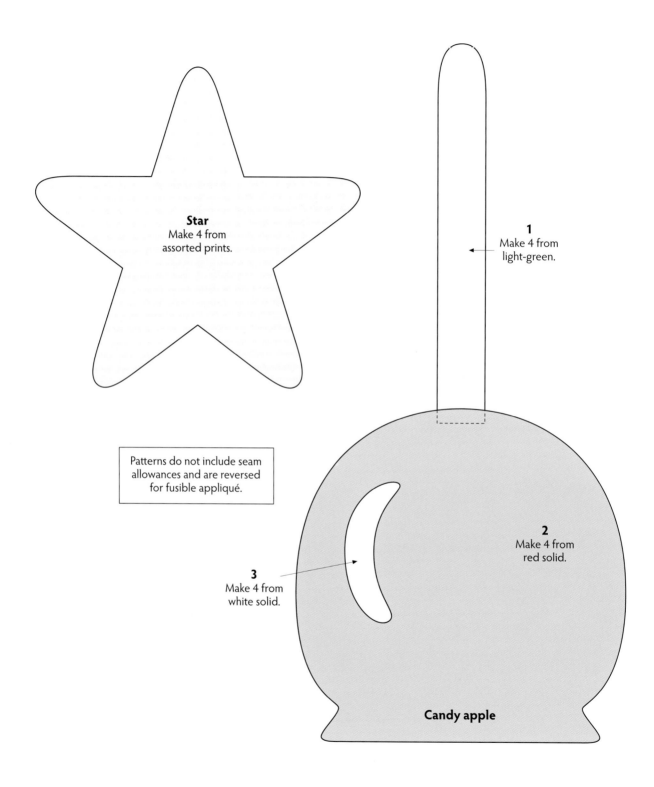

Star
Make 4 from
assorted prints.

1
Make 4 from
light-green.

Patterns do not include seam
allowances and are reversed
for fusible appliqué.

2
Make 4 from
red solid.

3
Make 4 from
white solid.

Candy apple

Berry Pillow and Pincushion

Designed and made by Jessi Jung

No matter what time of year it is, these delicious berries are always in season. Make the large version for fun round pillows, or the miniature version for cute little pincushions. The methods are practically the same.

BERRY PILLOW

FINISHED SIZE: 8" diameter

MATERIALS

Yardage is based on 42"-wide fabric unless otherwise noted. Yields 1 pillow.

½ yard of berry tone-on-tone print for pillow
5 squares, 10" x 10", of green print for leaves
1 square, 5" x 5", of purple floral for button
16-ounce bag of polyester fiberfill
Coordinating heavy-duty thread for leaves
1 covered button, 1⅞" diameter
Freezer paper
Long doll-making needle
Compass for drawing circles

MAKING THE PILLOW

1. Trace the berry pillow pattern on page 79 onto the dull side of a piece of freezer paper. Cut on the traced line to make a freezer-paper template.

2. Fold the ½ yard of berry print in half lengthwise, right sides together and raw edges aligned. Align the straight edge of the template with the fold on the fabric and use a pencil to trace six shapes. Cut out the shapes on the traced line. *Do not* cut along the fold. On each shape, mark a dot ¼" from each tip as shown on the pattern.

Fold.

3. With right sides together and using a ¼" seam allowance, pin and sew together two pieces from step 2, starting and stopping at the dots with a backstitch. Press the seam allowances in one direction.

4. Sew a third piece to the unit from step 3, starting and stopping at the dots with a backstitch to make half of the pillow. Press the seam allowances in the same direction as before. In the same way, sew the remaining three pieces together to make the other half of the pillow.

5. With right sides together, pin and sew the two pillow halves together, leaving a 4" opening at the top of one seam for turning.

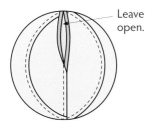

Leave open.

6. Turn the pillow right side out. Firmly stuff the pillow with fiberfill to make a full circular shape. Slip-stitch the opening closed. (The stitching will be concealed by the leaves.)

ADDING THE LEAVES

1. Use a compass to draw a 10"-diameter circle on the wrong side of each green square. Cut out the fabric circles on the drawn lines. Fold each circle in half and then in half again as shown.

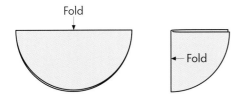

Fold

Fold

2. To make the leaf unit, thread a needle with a 36" length of heavy-duty thread and knot the ends together. Sew a continuous running stitch along the raw edges of the five folded circles. Pull the thread to gather the circles. Stitch the last circle to the first one, keeping the thread taut. Wrap the thread tightly, in and out between the circles, and tugging on the thread to close the center hole. Knot the thread and hide the knot under the leaf unit.

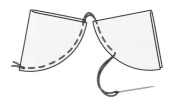

3. Follow the manufacturer's instructions to cover the button with the purple floral square.

Needle Grabber

Use a rubber jar opener to help grab and pull a needle through thick projects.

4. Thread a doll-making needle with heavy-duty thread and knot the ends together. Starting at the bottom center of the pillow, bring your needle up through the pillow to the top center. Insert the needle through the leaf unit and through the button shank. Then insert the needle back down through the leaves and pillow center. Pull the thread very tightly to give the leaves and button a snug fit. Make several more stitches to firmly attach the leaves and button. Knot the thread beneath the leaves and clip the thread.

BERRY PINCUSHION

FINISHED SIZE: 3" diameter

MATERIALS

Yields 1 pincushion.

1 square, 10" x 10", of berry tone-on-tone print for pincushion
3 squares, 5" x 5", of assorted prints for the leaves
1 ladybug button
Polyester fiberfill
Coordinating heavy-duty thread for leaves
Freezer paper
Long doll-making needle
Compass for drawing circles

MAKING THE PINCUSHION

For details and illustrations about the following techniques, refer to "Making the Pillow" on page 75 and "Adding the Leaves" on page 77.

1. Trace the berry pincushion pattern on page 79 onto the dull side of a piece of freezer paper. Cut on the traced line to make a freezer-paper template.

2. Use a pencil to trace six shapes on the wrong side of the berry print 10" square. Cut out the shapes on the traced line. On each shape, mark a dot ¼" from each tip as shown on the pattern.

3. Referring to steps 3–5 of "Making the Pillow," sew the shapes together to make the pincushion, leaving a 1½" opening at the top of one side for turning.

4. Turn the pincushion right side out. Firmly stuff the pincushion with fiberfill to make a full circular shape. Slip-stitch the opening closed.

5. Use a compass to draw a 5"-diameter circle on the wrong side of each print 5" square. Cut out the fabric circles on the drawn lines. Fold each circle in half and then in half again as shown on page 77.

6. Refer to steps 2 and 4 of "Adding the Leaves" to make a leaf unit. Sew the leaf unit and ladybug button to the pincushion.

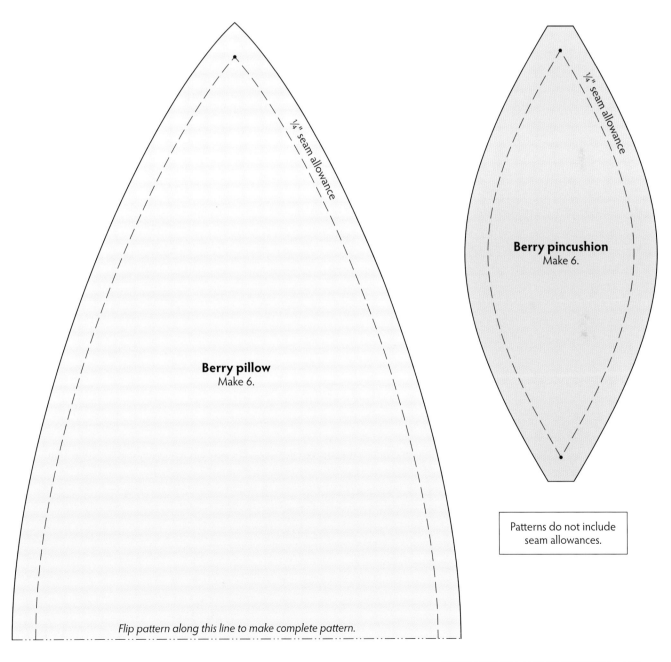

Berry pillow
Make 6.

¼" seam allowance

Flip pattern along this line to make complete pattern.

Berry pincushion
Make 6.

¼" seam allowance

Patterns do not include
seam allowances.

About the Authors

From left: Jessi Jung, Carrie Jung, and Lauren Jung

Lauren + Jessi Jung Designs is a family operation. We're a mother-and-two-daughters team with a passion for fabric, color, and sewing. Jessi (the mother) and Carrie, the company's pattern designers, have been dreaming up quilting and sewing patterns for a combined 10 years.

Lauren + Jessi Jung Designs got its start in the quilting and sewing industry as a fabric design team for Moda Fabrics, where credits have included five fabric lines and multiple quilt patterns. Taking much of their inspiration from nature, Lauren, a graphic designer and website developer, and Jessi, a longtime quilter and sewist, combine their talents to produce fresh and modern designs that appeal to a wide range of fabric enthusiasts. Later Carrie joined the team as well, making projects to show off the fabric line.

The L+J design team lives and works on opposite ends of the country and credit the wonders of modern technology for making their design process possible. Jessi lives in Spartanburg, South Carolina, Carrie works out of Albuquerque, New Mexico, and Lauren lives in San Francisco, California.

Visit their website at laurenandjessijung.com.

What's your creative passion?

Find it at **ShopMartingale.com**

books • eBooks • ePatterns • daily blog • free projects
videos • tutorials • inspiration • giveaways

Martingale®
Create with Confidence